introduction

The self-styled centre of the universe – if something's worth doing, you can do it here. Basically, West is classy, East is gritty and North and South are either crap or fantastic depending on which side of the river you live. Unfeasibly large, London will take you the rest of your life to get to know – still, everyone's got to start somewhere. itchy takes you through the myriad of entertainment on offer, from the cosiest of locals to the flashiest of style bars. Knees up mother Brown, I'm coming in...

© itchy Ltd
Globe Quay
Globe Road
Leeds
LS11 5QG
t: 0113 246 0440 f: 0113 246 0550
e: all@itchymedia.co.uk
www.itchycity.co.uk

ISBN 1-903753-11-2

City Managers: Emma Howarth, Mike Waugh **Editorial Team:** Simon Gray, Ruby Quince, Andrew Wood **Design:** Matt Wood **Cover Design:** ArtScience.net
Maps: Steve Cox at Crumb Eye Design
Contributors: Lee Coan, Sarah Ellison, Ruth Francis, Caroline Joy, Katherine Packer, Lousie Palmer, Meera Patel, Pete Sharman, Ramsay Short, Luci Smallwood, Sam Spurgeon, Rachel Williams, Ian Winterton
Photography: Antoinette, Jeff Knowles, Sam Spurgeon (www.photorepublic.co.uk/sam), Katharyn Quince
Acknowledgments: Joe Barry, Eamon Harkin, Lisa Parry, Alex Radford, Sally Robinson, Ruth Strothers
Jamie Oliver pictures copyright David Loftus

contents

Soho 6

Noho & Fitzrovia 18

Covent Garden .. 24

Leicester Square & Piccadilly 34

Camden 44

Islington 50

Hoxton & Shoreditch 58

Farringdon & Clerkenwell 66

Brixton 72

Clapham 80

Fulham 88

Notting Hill 96

Out of our areas 102

Gay 108

Entertainment .. 112
- Cinemas
- Theatres
- Snooker & Pool
- Strip Joints
- Art
- Comedy
- Museums
- Tourist
- Casinos
- 24-hour London
- Sport

Shopping 124

Body 138

Accommodation 142

Getting About .. 144

Index 146

Tube Map 149

london area map

NOT TO SCALE

RIVER THAMES

This map is designed to give you an idea of the geography of the city. But I wouldn't use it to get around, you'll get lost.

There are 12 detailed maps throughout the book, one at the beginning of each section.

MAP INDEX

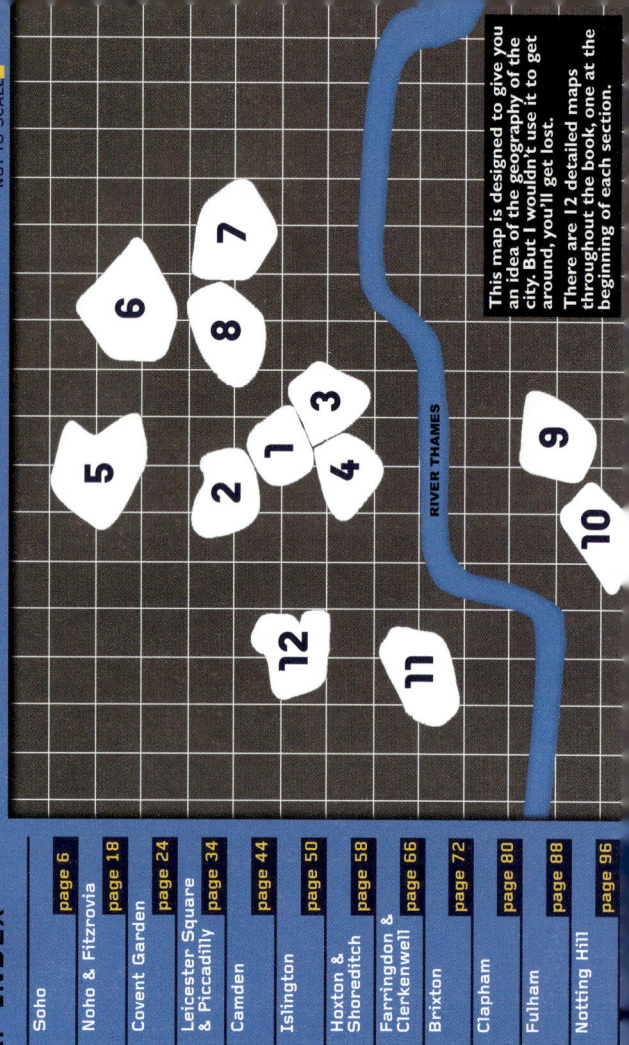

1. Soho — page 6
2. Noho & Fitzrovia — page 18
3. Covent Garden — page 24
4. Leicester Square & Piccadilly — page 34
5. Camden — page 44
6. Islington — page 50
7. Hoxton & Shoreditch — page 58
8. Farringdon & Clerkenwell — page 66
9. Brixton — page 72
10. Clapham — page 80
11. Fulham — page 88
12. Notting Hill — page 96

foreword

Jamie Oliver

London's a huge city with so much choice it's sometimes difficult to know where to look. That's why this itchy guide is so good – with a mixture of everything that London has to offer, from the best clubs to cracking record shops, you can't go far wrong! And at long last, someone's cottoned on to the fact that once in a while a dodgy pub and a bit of karaoke, beats posing at the latest bar opening, hands down.

I'm always flitting around the country, so all their guides come in useful at some stage. But for London, I had to persuade them to to squeeze in a couple of my favourite places that I thought were worth a mention. Check for the symbol.

It's reassuring to know that itchy take their research seriously. I know from experience that they certainly know how to mix business with pleasure.

– Jamie Oliver

Throughout the restaurant section, we've given the price of a meal for two. This is based on the price of a recommended dish for two people and a bottle of house wine. They should be used as a guide only!

For what's happening right here, right now and in 17 other cities... **www.itchycity.co.uk**. All the events, all the time, with news on gigs, cinema, restaurants, clubs and more. You can sign up for updates on anything from hip hop to happy hours, vent your anger about our reviews and get discounts for your favourite venues. Whatever's happening in the city, itchycity's there.

And for when you're out, we've made that hulking great big wap-phone actually useful. Next time it's 1am and you're gasping for a Guinness, whip out the wap and find your nearest late bar... **wap.itchycity.co.uk**

itchycity.co.uk

soho

www.itchycity.co.uk

Get rich, get famous and get yourself a pad in Soho for twenty-four hour entertainment. Get a bit older, start complaining to the council about the noise and ruin it for the rest of us. It's not exactly easy to open somewhere new, or secure a late licence in these parts anymore – but it hasn't affected the ambience. Soho basically *is* London nightlife.

Bars

Abigail's Party

25-27 Brewer St, W1
(020) 7434 2911 Piccadilly Circus

Members' bars? Wall to wall pretty people wittering on about how cool they are? No thanks. Abigail's Party does its

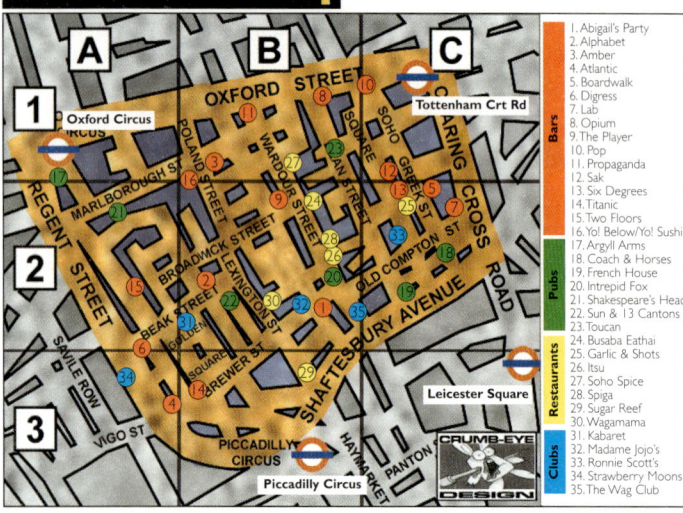

Bars
1. Abigail's Party
2. Alphabet
3. Amber
4. Atlantic
5. Boardwalk
6. Digress
7. Lab
8. Opium
9. The Player
10. Pop
11. Propaganda
12. Sak
13. Six Degrees
14. Titanic
15. Two Floors
16. Yo! Below/Yo! Sushi

Pubs
17. Argyll Arms
18. Coach & Horses
19. French House
20. Intrepid Fox
21. Shakespeare's Head
22. Sun & 13 Cantons
23. Toucan

Restaurants
24. Busaba Eathai
25. Garlic & Shots
26. Itsu
27. Soho Spice
28. Spiga
29. Sugar Reef
30. Wagamama

Clubs
31. Kabaret
32. Madame Jojo's
33. Ronnie Scott's
34. Strawberry Moons
35. The Wag Club

www.itchylondon.co.uk

best to break the mould and we'd go as far as saying it's a damned good laugh. There's no making up for the fact that getting invited onto their members' list is the social equivalent of climbing Mount Everest in flip-flops, but for a night of decadence in luxurious surroundings it's near perfect. Make friends with the lovely Abigail (yes, she really is called Abigail) and get your cheque-book out.
Mon-Sat 6-2
Membership £70 a year.

Alphabet
61-63 Beak St, W1
(020) 7439 2190 ⊖ **Oxford Circus**
Grab a drink and head straight downstairs. Recline on old car seats, play Space Invaders, relive your youth but with a higher quality of beverage. Smuggling in a

two-litre bottle of White Lightening will be frowned upon, and is frankly taking things a touch too far. Alphabet really captures that Soho feeling; ad execs mingle with shop girls, DJs with media types, all having way too good a time to bother networking. Just the way we like it.
Mon-Fri 12-11, Sat 5-11
Meal for two: £30 (Seared tuna steak) evening menu is bar snacks only.

Amber
6 Poland St, W1 (020) 7734 3094
⊖ **Oxford Circus**
All new from the good folk of Alphabet. Amber attracts a similar and slightly more sophisticated crowd. With its earthy interior, DJs and Brazilian menu, Amber is the kind of place you'll go to for a change of scene, and return to because you love it.
Mon-Fri 11-1, Sat 5-1 Admission after 11, £3
Meal for two: £26 (Chicken and chorizo stew)

Atlantic Bar & Grill
20 Glasshouse St, W1 (020) 7734 4888
⊖ **Piccadilly Circus**
Fancy feeling really ugly, poor and unimportant? Well, look no further. Atlantic still lives off the celebrity hangout status acquired in its formative days. There's a fair few A/B/C listers still kicking around and if that's your thing and you're loaded you'll probably love it here. Otherwise, avoid like the plague. The décor is impressive, amazingly high ceilings and sweeping stairs – but when you can't quite shake the feeling that you belong under a rock, is it really worth it?
Mon-Fri 12-3, Sat 5-3, Sun 6-10.30
Meal for two: £50 (Rack of Welsh lamb), bar snacks also available.

THE INDEPENDENT   www.independent.co.uk

Boardwalk

18 Greek St, W1
(020) 7287 2051 ⊖ **Tottenham Ct Rd**
Lends itself to all kinds of drunken debauchery, no poncing around sipping cocktails here. It's more of a line 'em up and get 'em down you kind of a place. Fun and totally devoid of cool kids and Soho posers, so in that way a decent place. Exclusive it is not, so those seeking a more glamourous night out and an opportunity to schmooze with London's glitterati should look further afield.
Mon-Sat 4-3, Admission Mon £3, Fri/Sat after 11pm, £5
Meal for two: £37 (Char grilled fillet steak)

Digress

10 Beak St, W1
(020) 7437 0239 ⊖ **Piccadilly Circus**
Just off Regent St in deepest West Soho, some people think that Sydney is the capital of Australia when in fact it's Canberra, but I digress. This place fits the bill for a no hassle drinking session. Often quieter than the rest of its Soho neighbours but they don't hide the fact – there's an intriguing counter above the exit allowing you to keep tabs on exactly how many people have graced their doors. Now, divide that by double your own attractiveness rating out of ten and

times by four – that's your chances of pulling. Extra points if there's a hen or stag party in, and there often is.
Mon-Wed 12-late, Thu-Sat 12-3
Admission Mon-Thu £3 after 11, Fri/Sat after 10 £5
Meal for two: £22 (Vegetarian sushi, bar snacks menu)

Lab

12 Old Compton St, W1 (020) 7437 7820
⊖ **Tottenham Court Rd**
A street of a thousand bars, yet Lab manages to stand out in both design and atmosphere. On two levels, both the ground floor and basement have a distinct, seventies Rainbow feel about them, minus the ambiguous sexual preference scandals. Given we're on Old Compton St, the Lab's clientele are shockingly straight. Top-notch bar staff and potent cocktails.
Mon-Sat 12-12, Sun 5-10.30
Meal for two: £26 (Thai green curry)

Opium

1a Dean St, W1
(020) 7287 9608 ⊖ **Tottenham Ct Rd**

New bars are opening faster than we can keep track of, and this one seems to be receiving a lot of attention. Oriental, luxurious interior, late licence and a central location. Bound to end up as one of those places you just can't ever get into.
Mon-Fri 12-3.30, Sat 7.30-3.30
Admission Tue/Sat after 10.30 £15
Meal for two: £52 (Oriental seabass)

The Player

8-12 Broadwick St, W1
(020) 7494 9125 ⊖ **Oxford Circus**

Leather seated, slightly sleazy, loungey kind of place. Somewhere I imagine would make a marvellous meeting place for a reunion with the boys from school. Extremely popular, laid back and with an understated elegance. Watch out for the waiter, apparently they call him 'the player from The Player', got to be a bit sinister that one.
Mon-Thu 6-12, Fri 6-1, Sat 8-1

Pop

14 Soho St, W1
(020) 7734 4004 ⊖ **Tottenham Ct Rd**

A lighting showroom crossed with Pat Sharpe's fun house. Sky high prices, condescending bar-staff and one of those cordoned-off VIP areas, so if you're deigned important enough to sit behind the blue rope you can keep an eye on the little people. How marvellous. It does boast the first female urinal in London – mildly intriguing I suppose... well actually no.
Mon-Thu 5-3.30, Fri 5-4, Sat 8-5

Propaganda

201 Wardour St, W1 (020) 7434 3820
⊖ **Tottenham Court Rd**

Just opened in the wake of Reggie Reggie's Soul Café, Propaganda is the new kid on the Soho block. With a massive capacity, late licence, slick design and random indoor garden it should turn out to be a popular one. Poptastically, Five had their end of tour party here. Which should make you get down. Watch this space.
Mon-Thurs 5-3, Fri/Sat 5-3

Sak

49 Greek St, W1 (020) 7439 4159
⊖ **Leicester Sq/Tottenham Court Rd**

Ok, so you're prepared. You know it'll be hard to get in and the doormen are supremely arsey, you're psyched up with names to drop and ready for the

onslaught, and then they go and let you in. Just like that and bloody smile while they're at it. Saks lost its attitude before we even got a chance to slag it off. Gutted. It is expensive, but other than that it's nice, stylish and not too packed at the weekend.
Mon-Tue 5.30-2, Wed-Sat 4.30-3, Admission Fri/Sat after 10.30pm £5
Bar snacks: from £3 (pizzettas)

TOP FIVE...
Late drinks (no door tax)
1. Brixtonian Havana (p73)
2. Titanic (p10)
3. Ice House (p52)
4. Cafe Sol (p81)
5. S'ditch Elec Sh'rm (p60)

Six Degrees

56 Frith St, W1
(020) 7734 8300 Piccadilly Circus
This place is pretty swanky with a fancy restaurant and glamourous members lounge. The downstairs bar is spacious and relaxed with a fantastic, glass waterfall at the entrance. After all, what's a bar without an elaborate, indoor water feature, hmm? Anyhow, Six Degrees is a great place to feel sophisticated without a staid atmosphere. Kylie had her last birthday party here, danced on the tables and rumour has it you can still see her fingerprints on the mirrors.
Mon-Sat, 12-11, the upstairs bar is open 'til 1am for those who've eaten in the restaurant.
Meal for two: £39 (Grilled calves liver)

Titanic

81 Brewer St, W1
(020) 7437 1912 Piccadilly Circus
There's something I love about Titanic and I think it's the fact that it's gone downhill. It used to be super-cool and exclusive and now it's, well, not. The doormen retain the pretence of selective admittance, but the once trendy movers and shakers have been replaced by drunken, home-counties divorcees and badly dressed Euro trash. And they let me in, in flip-flops. Swirl through the red revolving doors into a world of pure ostentation, sign your credit card receipt without looking and subtlety molest the person next to you – honestly the place is hilarious. I implore you all, to help make Titanic the most popular joint in town. If it's good enough for Jerry Springer, it's good enough for us.
Mon 5.30-1 (bar snacks only) Tue-Sat 5.30-11 (restaurant) bar open 'til 3am
Meal for two: £40 (Grilled plaice with new potatoes)

Two Floors

3 Kingly St, W1 (020) 7439 1007
 Piccadilly Circus
Oh aren't we cool, all battered old sofas

and intimidatingly beautiful bar staff. So cool in fact, we don't even need a sign above the door. No one really just happens upon Two Floors, but check it out and you'll probably find you'll come back for more. Everyone looks like they know each other, and it's easy to feel that you've stumbled upon a private party, but the atmosphere is decidedly chilled.
Mon-Sat 11-11
Daytime sandwiches: Ciabatta £4

Yo! Below

52 Poland St, W1
(020) 7287 0443 ⊖ **Oxford Circus**

Hi-tech, novel bar with free massages, sunken seating and self service beer on tap. Get a table with some mates and do your worst. The bar staff are selected for their singing abilities which is a relief when the impromtu karaoke starts later on. Not a place for pulling, though the waitresses will happily send over your number on a napkin if you so desire, but an excellent stress-free night out.
Mon-Tue 12-11, Wed-Sat 12-1, Sun 5-10.30 Admission £3 after 11

Pubs

Argyll Arms

18 Argyll St (020) 7734 6117
⊖ **Oxford Circus**
A bit of a tourist trap due to its location just off Oxford St but it's a good traditional pub, worth a visit if you can handle the hordes. Also makes a handy meeting place for gathering friends together before heading deeper into Soho. Better than meeting outside the Aberdeen Steakhouse in the rain anyway.

Coach & Horses

29 Greek St (020) 7437 5920
⊖ **Leicester Sq/Tottenham Court Rd**
Real, proper, Soho boozer for folks who don't like ponceing about with bizarre foreign lagers. Order a pint and make like a regular. Talk is tough, smoke fills the air and the last one out is a hero. For pub lovers desperate for a retreat from central London's style bars, this is a godsend.

you've tried this one...now try them all 17 other cities to indulge in

soho   11

French House

49 Dean St, W1 (020) 7437 2799
🚇 **Piccadilly Circus/Leicester Square**
Perhaps the most famous Soho pub, and a favourite meeting place of many a grand British intellect over the decades, including Francis Bacon and Dylan Thomas. The French House is quirky and charming and its clientele the same. Busy at the oddest hours of the day, and when you make it to the bar through the haze of cigarette smoke you'll find the landlord will only serve you lager in halves. Eccentric but truly English.

Intrepid Fox

99 Wardour St, W1 (020) 7287 8359
🚇 **Leicester Sq**
You either fit in here or you don't. Those without a heavy metal t-shirt, excess of body hair and muscles built up through years of carrying amps for obscure devil worshipping bands – you won't. It has a weird Halloween feel every night of the year and is immensely popular partly due to its status as a one-time punk meeting place and the fact that there really is nowhere else quite like it. Go on, dust off your steel toe-capped boots and give it a go.

Shakespeare's Head

29, Great Marlborough St, W1
(020) 7734 2911
Big, traditional pub just off Carnaby St. Not meaning to brag but I once spotted Gruey, you know from the eighties kids TV show of the same name, sipping a snakebite and black by the bar? It could happen to you.

Sun & Thirteen Cantons

21 Great Pulteney St, W1
(020) 7734 0934
🚇 **Oxford Circus/Piccadilly Circus**
Pub with a clubby vibe, packed with the youth of today being insolent and rude about the war and old folk. Give it a wide berth if you're in any way getting on a bit or get confused about all that modern music the young 'uns are into these days. This pub is young, fun, chilled out and the bar-staff tell some good jokes.

Toucan

19 Carlisle St, W1 (020) 7437 4123
🚇 **Tottenham Court Rd**
One of the best taverns in Soho. It's not the littlest pub in the area – that accolade goes to The Dog & Duck – but it is small, and small as the saying goes is

beautiful. Cosy, full of old-timers, and arguably serves the best Guinness in London. And if you like your whisky Irish it's got over 50 different brands to choose from. Perfect.

Restaurants

Busaba Eathai

106-110 Wardour St, W1 (020) 7255 8686
Tottenham Crt Rd/Piccadilly Circus
Check out the queues. Yes it's good, and yes it's worth the wait. We promise. The mastermind behind the Wagamama concept makes good once more with a modern take on Thai. Good value, stylish venue, with amazing, but not scarily authentic food. The large tables mean maximum socialising with your fellow diners. Like Thailand but better.
Mon-Thu 12-11, Fri-Sat 12-11.30, Sun 12-10
Meal for two: £24 (Chilli prawn stir fry)

Garlic & Shots

14 Frith St, W1 (020) 7734 9505
Leicester Sq/Tottenham Court Rd
The only place Buffy will eat out when she's filming in London. My, you'd be a foolish vampire to set foot in this den of garlic iniquity. Literally everything is available in garlic; beer, ice-cream, the lot. Now, you could see this as a shrewd move, ideal for avoiding that first date bad breath nightmare, or as a slightly worrying place likely to attract freaks. We recommend treating the regulars with suspicion. It's nothing if not interesting and has a startling array of rock-hard vodka shots.
Mon-Wed 5-12, Thu-Sat 6-1, Sun 5-11.30
Meal for two: £25 (Garlic red extra hot chilli)

Itsu

103 Wardour St, W1 (020) 7479 4794
Leicester Sq/Tottenham Court Rd
Yo! Sushi's prettier, less hi-tech second cousin, twice removed, from the posh side of town. A classy take on conveyor belt sushi, but still with that nerve wracking, waiting-for-your-suitcase-at-the-airport feeling, no matter how many times you tell yourself it's just food. Albeit award-winning.
Mon-Sun 12-3.30 then 6-11
Meal for two: £22 (Sushi)

www.itchylondon.co.uk

Who are you?
Sue, 30, Art Director, lives Whitechapel
Tequila's on me. Where to? Bar Vinyl
Cool. Now I'm starving... Ok, Souk then. The food's amazing.
But I'm easily bored. Take me clubbing.
Let's go to Fabric or the Gardening Club
Want to run away to Mexico with me?
No I love London. It's so diverse
Bet you hate the tube though? Well, yes

Soho Spice
124-126 Wardour St, W1 (020) 7434 0808
Piccadilly Circus/Tottenham Court Rd
Contemporary Indian dishes amid vibrant surroundings. Now, naturally it lacks that rough and ready appeal of your traditional curry house, but once you've overcome the temptation to down ten pints and chant rugby songs, you'll have a great time. The menu changes regularly featuring dishes from all sorts of obscure regions – cast your mind back to that gap-year voyage of discovery – and rest assured it'll be nothing like it.
Mon-Thu 12-12.30, Fri-Sat 12-3
Meal for two: £35 (Chicken tikka masala)

Spiga
84-86 Wardour St, W1 (020) 7734 3444
Tottenham Court Rd
A good choice for a nice bit of Italian in central London. Spiga's been around for a while and still comes up with the goods. Great and not overly costly pizza and pasta dishes in buzzingly loud surroundings. Packed with youthful folk enjoying their wood-fired al funghi with gusto.
Mon-Tue 12-3 then 6-11, Wed-Sat 12-3 then 6-12, Sun 12-3 then 6-11
Meal for two: £29 (Pizza fresca)

Sugar Reef
42-44 Great Windmill St, W1
(020) 7851 0800
Piccadilly Circus

The giant disco ball outside gives some indication as to what you can expect beyond the scary door policy. Larger than life and favoured for nights out by such luminaries as Billie Piper and Martine McC, Sugar Reef is pricey, over the top and sadly not that much fun. Food is Pacific Rim, I ask you.
Mon-Sat 12-3 then 6-12.30
Meal for two: £51 (Roast lemon sole)

Find places for late drinks on your WAP
wap.itchylondon.co.uk

www.itchylondon.co.uk

Wagamama

10a Lexington St, W1 (020) 7292 0990
⊖ Oxford Circus

The kind of place that makes you feel instantly inefficient and inspired to start organising your life with military precision. The service is excellent, staff take your order on hand-held computers and everything arrives freshly cooked and immaculately presented. Healthy, one dish, Japanese noodles and rice, and no special treatment. Wagamama's is totally egalitarian, whether you're Robbie Williams or the managing director of the company you'll have to queue...busy and deserving of its popularity. Fast turnover and worth the shorter-than-you'd-think wait for a seat.
Mon-Thu 12-11, Fri-Sat 12-12, Sun 12.30-10

Meal for two: £24 (Chilli chicken ramen)

Yo! Sushi

52 Poland St, W1 (020) 7287 0443
⊖ Oxford Circus

Instantly inspires Generation Game style amusement as you test your mates on what comes round the conveyor belt. Extra points for remembering the items that no one ever takes off, obscure little pots of flaky things inevitably. A novel take on fast food apart from someone a few tables ahead always grabs that dish of sashimi you had your eye on. Don't start a fight – it's not very Japanese (Pearl Harbour anyone? - Ed).
Mon-Sun 12-12

Meal for two: £16 (Sushi)

Clubs

Kabaret

5 Upper St John St, W1 (020) 7287 8140
⊖ Piccadilly Circus

When Kate Moss wants to show off her new haircut she gets in a limo and heads for Kabaret. This tiny Soho club has been around for aeons and has enjoyed a celebrity renaissance in recent years. Small and dark, it's fairly easy to see the appeal. Don't even attempt to get in on a Thursday unless you've graced the cover of Harpers & Queen or your Dad owns a publishing empire. Friday and Saturday are slightly more relaxed, call ahead and ask to put your name on the list. There are a few changes in the pipeline, with the club looking at increasing its opening and going back to its cabaret roots. Still, it'll never be worth bothering on an ugly day.

Madame JoJo's
8 Brewer St, W1 (020) 7734 3040
Piccadilly Circus/Leicester Square

Moving away from cabaret, well slightly, Madame JoJo's has recently launched a myriad of new club nights, from disco to funky house. The venue has had a refurb, the sound systems have been upgraded and things are looking pretty good. Still, drag show devotees needn't despair, the Saturday night show remains untainted by the winds of change, and is still a top night out.

Ronnie Scott's
47 Frith St, W1 (020) 7430 0747
Tottenham Court Rd

The original super-cool jazz club. Extremely popular, with a sophisticated crowd of serious music lovers, attracted to the chilled atmosphere and quality acts. This place attracts the best musicians of the genre and it's best to book a seat in advance. The crowd is an older one and it's not really the kind of place where you'll throw your empties over your shoulder, but if jazz is your thing you'll absolutely love it.

Strawberry Moons
15 Heddon St, W1 (020) 7437 7300
Piccadilly Circus

Just outside the boundaries of Soho, but near enough to include and worth a mention for its shameless celebration of supreme tackiness. Attracts a mixture of students, raucously drunken office workers, and graduates wanting to relive those retro nights down the union. Cool London it ain't. The kind of place you'd brag about being on the guest list for? Not that either. But for 100% naff party tunes and an easy pull it's the greatest thing to happen to W1 in a long, long time.

The Wag Club
35 Wardour St, W1 (020) 7437 5534
Piccadilly Circus/Tottenham Crt Rd

Most famed for its Saturday night, mod-

Hot tip

extravaganza, Blow Up where modern day sixties kids line the walls, sporting heavy eyeliner, sharp mod suits and sullen expressions. The rest of the week offers a joyous melange of 70s/80s and indie rock nights, suiting the dark, dingy surroundings and angst ridden (apart from when we're dancing ironically to Duran Duran) clientele just fine.

Illicit drinking

OK, so you're staggering around the West End, desperate for another drink. Queues are too long or expensive to bother with, and you think there must be somewhere else. Outside the licensed venues, there is, but this is where you might come a cropper. A knock on the door, an ominous bouncer, and a cover charge of anywhere between £5 and £20 will grant you entry into the most scary night of your life.

Around the Tottenham Court area, and we obviously can't say exactly where, there are a few places which rope in unsuspecting newcomers to the city and fleece them for all they're worth. Upon entering, you'll be greeted by weed, crack, skag and just about every other illicit substance your mother warned you about. At this point, some lads will be thinking it can't be that bad, I can handle myself blah blah blah. Well, no matter how hard you think you are, there will always be one junkie-crazed mad-eye-balled loony who'll make sure that yes, you do want that luke warm can of Red Stripe for a tenner, and oh yes, you'll take five, and while you're about it, why not offer a Christmas tip? Before I blade you? Not for the faint-hearted or sane-minded.

After hours...
on the move
wap.itchylondon.co.uk

RIZLA+ It's what you make of it.

soho 17

noho & fitzrovia

www.itchycity.co.uk

Bars

Bradley's Spanish Bar
42-44 Hanway St, W1 (020) 7636 0359
Tottenham Court Rd

Immensely popular Spanish bar; a veritable institution. Set yourself up for the evening with a couple of San Miguels. Then keep on going amid friendly banter with the bizarre mix that fill this bar every evening. It does get busy, but in a good, mingling kind of way, and the jukebox is amongst London's finest. The only shocker is that they recently stopped doing food altogether so you'll have to make do with liquid sustenance. Piddly little bowls of deep-fried crustacea never really did it for me anyway.
Mon-Sat 11-11

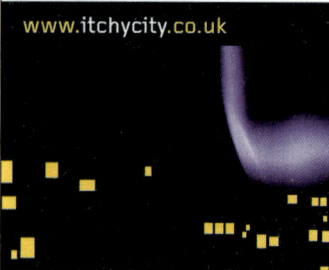

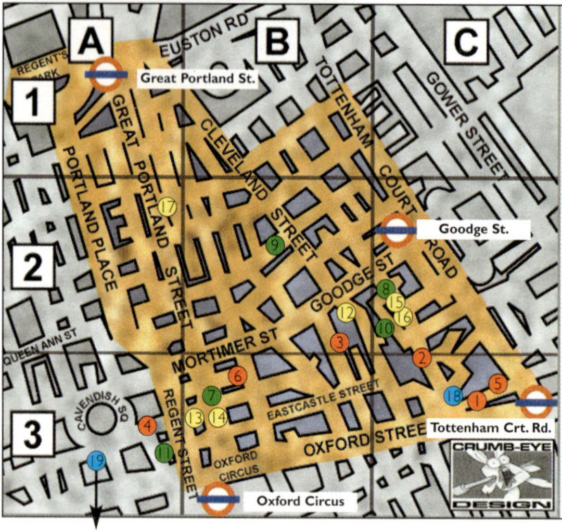

Bars
1. Bradley's Spanish Bar
2. Jerusalem
3. Long Bar
4. Match
5. Sevilla Mia
6. The Social

Pubs
7. Cock Tavern
8. Fitzroy Tavern
9. King & Queen
10. Newman Arms
11. The Old Explorer

Restaurants
12. Dish Dash
13. The Kerala
14. Mash
15. Passione
16. Rasa
17. Villandry

Clubs
18. The Office
19. Loop

Jerusalem
33-34 Rathbone Place, W1
(020) 7255 1120 ⊖ **Tottenham Ct Rd**
This massive underground bar is a fine choice for after work or indeed anytime drinks. Massive wooden tables give it a school refectory feel, and deep red walls, curtains and candles an entirely different, glamorous one. Good DJs, attractive clientele, friendly bar and funky tunes. Always heavingly busy at night and it's no surprise – this place is cracking.
Mon-Thu 12pm-2am, Fri 12pm-3am, Sat 7pm-3am. Admission after 10.30, £3 Mon-Thu, £6 Fri-Sat
Late licence currently under review, but should be back in place by February
Meal for two: £28 (Sausage and mash)

Long Bar
Sanderson Hotel
50 Berners St, W1 (020) 7300 1400
⊖ **Oxford Circus**
It is indeed. If you're at this end of town and feeling flash, this is the latest 'in' bar. So posh it's frightening; the kind of place where you just know you're going to smash something or reveal your lack of class by yelling 'by eck it's flashy in 'ere innit?' Try not to, it really is a fantastic, glamorous place to spend a ridiculous amount on one drink. And you never know who you might meet (Gail Porter is a regular at the gym upstairs), if you can make that half last long enough.
Mon-Sat 10-1, Sun 10-10.30

Match
37-38 Margaret St, W1
(020) 7499 3443 ⊖ **Oxford Circus**
Delicious, colourful, but pricey cocktails and an overabundance of over-dressed office chicks. As a result, men seem to flock here – the kind of men that call girls 'ladies' and not in a joke way, but don't seem to mind getting their gold cards out in return for the pleasure of their company. That all sounds a bit negative but it isn't intended to be. Match is (if you remove its patrons) a classy venue that inspires the best kind of night out, the kind that starts with a couple of bottles of Budvar and ends in B52s all round and a dodgy taxi home. If Match strikes a chord – and that's a good line to take us to the bottom of the page – you'll find venues in Shoreditch and Clerkenwell too.
Mon-Sat 11-12
Meal for two: £22 (Nachos)

Sevilla Mia

22 Hanway St, W1 (020) 7637 3756
 Oxford Circus

Hanway St is the West End's little Spanish hideaway. And the cramped, crumbling, basement bar that is Sevilla Mia is its jewel in the crown, recognisable only by a tacky white and red sign above the door, which makes you think more of a Soho den of iniquity. Friendly staff serving San Miguel and Alhambra beer, delicious tapas and undoubtedly your best bet: potent jugs of fruity sangria. The bar's highlight is its ageing guitarist, there every night, offering vocal flamenco yet always managing to look grumpy. More Andalucia than central London, early arrival is a must to get a seat amongst the eccentric crowd of eurohippies and Spanish exiles.
Mon-Sat 7-1, Sun 7-12

The Social

5 Little Portland St, W1
(020) 7636 4992 Oxford Circus

A good all rounder. Cosy booths, spacious basement, cool design, casual feel. But it does have slightly irritating retro bar snacks, I can knock up a perfectly good bit of cheese on toast at home, thank you very much. Still, this kind of comfort food holds a certain appeal. The narrow, upstairs bar is good if you grab a booth, and a bit too, well, narrow if you don't. Music's always spot on (dance, funk and house) and the clientele are your trendy trainer wearing, record bag carrying types. Always packed, especially at weekends, reflecting its loyal, and decidedly happy punters' desire to come back for more.
Mon-Sat 12-12, Sun 5-11

Bar snacks: From £2 (Eggy bread)

Pubs

Cock Tavern

27 Great Portland St, W1 (020) 7631 5002
Oxford Circus

Popular old-style pub filled with office workers. The outside tables and no nonsense attitude of the staff and punters make it a fine choice for a few swift pints on your way home from work. Especially the kind of few swift pints that turn into a few more not so swift ones.

Fitzroy Tavern

16 Charlotte St, W1 (020) 7580 3714
Goodge St

Another popular tavern that used to be frequented by Dylan Thomas and his range of foreign literary friends.

Nowadays, it's a place to eat, drink and make merry. Go forth, see if the literary skill that once inhabited it rubs off on you. Alternatively try your luck on the fruit machines.

King & Queen
I Foley St, W1 (020) 7636 5619
Goodge St
Totally traditional pub where we're told Bob Dylan once played. Two good reasons to give it a go. And if you do, you won't be disappointed. A good range of ales, decent pub grub and a jukebox of dubious quality. What more could you ask for?

Newman Arms
23 Rathbone St (020) 7636 1127
Goodge St
No-one will try and beat you up or flog you a knocked-off car stereo, but they might baffle you with talk of Excel spreadsheets and cashflow. Host to a crowd who are most at home on the IT helpdesk – handy, so use the phone number above for all your technical queries. A small, relaxed pub for when the bright lights of Oxford Street get that bit too bright. A good line in crisps too. Now there's a draw.

The Old Explorer
23 Gt Castle St, W1 (020) 7491 0467
Oxford Circus
A massive, two-level drinking den. As with any pub this size, there's no pretending you're down your local. You are definitely in central London, and you don't know anyone. Fine for a few drinks, and gathering up stray pub crawlers, not the kind of place to impress a hot date or linger.

Restaurants/Restaurant Bars

Dish Dash

jamie oliver rates...
57/59 Goodge St, W1 (020) 7637 7474
Goodge St
If you've never tried Peruvian food, then now's your chance. This place takes an interesting spin on your ordinary tapas, particularly for the veggies amongst you who are well catered for. It's a place designed for large parties, so get a bunch of your mates together and prepare yourself for some of the most interesting tucker in town. J.O.
Mon-Fri 12-12, Sat-Sun 6-12
Meal for two: £36 (Honey and chilli swordfish kebab)

The Kerala
15 Great Castle St, W1 (020) 7580 2125
Oxford Circus
Appears fairly average from the outside, but far from it and fully deserving of its popularity. Bargainous, well presented, Keralan food, in a restaurant with a truly

everything entertainment (except porn) www.itchylondon.co.uk

relaxed atmosphere. A small miracle given its proximity to the living hell that is Oxford St. Good for listening in on the latest Radio One gossip, it's just round the corner and a long-standing favourite with them crazy pop kids.
Mon-Sat 12-3 then 5.30-11
Meal for two: £20 (Vegetable Biryani)

Mash

19-21 Great Portland St, W1
(020) 7637 5555
⊖ **Oxford Circus**

Mash is a hugely popular three-in-one: Oliver Peyton restaurant above, a bar below and its own brewery. All of which combine to equal a fine evening's entertainment. The international mix of food is imaginative and it's expensive too, so it must be good. Mash is enormous and oozes a kind of slick, space-age cool whilst remaining unintimidating and friendly. The crowd tends towards suited office workers and trendy All Saints/ Robbie Williams wannabes, so go with a group of mates, get stuck into their range of beers and you'll have a great time. Until you check the photo wall at any rate – I'm still having flashbacks.
Mon-Sat 11-1, Sun 11-10.30pm
Meal for two: £40 (Whole roasted seabass)

Passione

10 Charlotte St, W1 (020) 7636 2833
⊖ **Goodge St**

A real hidden gem, and I'm not just saying that because the owners a mate! Fresh, homemade Italian with a great selection of antipasti and some seriously pukka fresh bread. I've never seen anywhere as dedicated to their mushrooms as this place. The owner pops down to Epping Forest and picks his own, and saves himself a packet in the process. All round one of the best places to eat in London. J.O.
Mon-Sat 12.30-2.30, 7-10.50
Meal for two: £45 (Sea bass)

Flick through the papers

Rasa

jamie oliver rates

5 Charlotte St, W1 (020) 7637 0222
⊖ Goodge St
(also in Stoke Newington and Dering St)
If you want genuinely authentic Indian cuisine then this is the one. Strictly vegetarian (except the Charlotte St branch which does seafood) the food comes all the way from the Kerala area in Southern India. I love my meat and two veg, but I don't mind giving it up for one night when the food's this good. The pickles and chutney are a real treat, but, to be honest you can't go wrong with anything on the menu. So good in fact that I had to work there for a while just to see how they do it. J.O.
Mon-Sat 12-3, 6-11 no lunch on Sunday
Meal for two: £23 (Cheera parippu curry)

Villandry

170 Great Portland St, W1 (020) 7631 3131
⊖ Great Portland St
A restaurant and delicatessen full of fascinating food stuffs — the kind of things you feel you should be far too young and hip to care about. Stuffed sun-dried tomatoes and things involving saffron. Drink some cider in the park afterwards to compensate.
Mon-Sun 8.30-10
Meal for two: £36 (Shoulder of lamb)

Clubs

The Office

3-5 Rathbone Place, W1 (020) 7636 1598
⊖ Tottenham Court Rd
In the main a bar, but doubling up enough as a club for us to include it here. The Office attracts hoards of young 'uns who come to make the most of happy hour, get pissed and snog each other. What are you waiting for... haven't we said enough? Take your tie off, hitch up your skirt, boogaloo and get on in there.

Loop

19 Dering Street, W1
(020) 7493 1003
⊖ Bond Street
Don't be deceived by the deceptively small pokey bar on the ground floor because underneath lies another world of the most happening tunes and a party crowd revelling like it's New Years Eve every night. Uh... no, it's not quite that good, but it's the best of a bad bunch around the area. The middle floor is kind of a loungy, chill-out mishmash of stools and velvet, while the simple dancefloor downstairs keeps the commercial dance lovers off the streets 'til a measly 1am on Thu, Fri and Sat. At which time you'll wonder where the hell to go next. You're screwed.

RIZLA+ www.rizla.com

covent garden

www.itchycity.co.uk

Covent Garden is one of those places that looks pretty but seems to lack substance. Packed with tourists, strange men with sandwich boards and street performers. If you're the kind of person who still finds those human statue acts amusing, you'll be in your element. If you're not, don't despair. There are some worthy places to spend your free time, you've just got to know where to find them.

Bars

Africa Bar
38 King St, WC2
(020) 7836 1976 ⊖ Covent Garden
Strange things are afoot at the Africa Bar. Turn up any night of the week and you'll

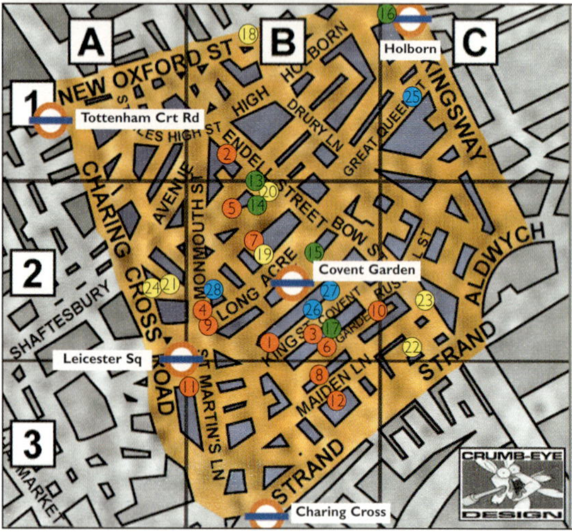

Bars
1. Africa Bar
2. Bibo Cibo
3. Covent Garden Wine Bar
4. Denim
5. Detroit
6. Fuel
7. The Langley
8. La Perla
9. Long Island Iced Tea Shop
10. Retox Bar
11. Saint
12. Spot

Pubs
13. The Crown & Anchor
14. Freedom Brewing Co.
15. The Nag's Head
16. Princess Louise
17. Punch & Judy

Restaurants
18. AKA/The End
19. Café Pacifico
20. Food for Thought
21. The Ivy
22. Joe Allen
23. Livebait
24. Souk

Clubs
25. Browns
26. The Gardening Club
27. The Rock Garden
28. Stringfellow's

24

invariably encounter all manner of bizarre dancing and a jubilant crowd. An interesting place to stop off on a bar crawl. African culture devotees and expats love it. And there's sure as hell nothing quite like it anywhere else in the capital. Check it out.
Mon-Thu 5.30-11, Fri-Sat 5.30-3

Bibo Cibo

59 Endell St, WC2 (020) 7240 3343
⊖ Covent Garden

New, stylish, drinking and eating den receiving your usual flurry of press attention. Seemingly, however, deserved of the hype. Simple, stylish and quirky, attracting a barrage of trendy drinkers, some of whom we're sure will stay put, even when the next big thing flings its doors open.
Mon-Sat 8-12, Sun 11-4

Meal for two: £30 (Roast chicken)

Covent Garden Wine Bar

1-2 The Piazza, WC2 (020) 7240 6654
⊖ Covent Garden

A boulevard wine bar with a truly

TOP FIVE...
Pulling – fussy
1. **Abigail's Party (p6)**
2. **Elbow Rooms (p51)**
3. **Six Degrees (p10)**
4. **Liquid Lounge (p97)**
5. **Langley (p26)**

Parisian feel? This isn't Paris, it's London. So, take away the fresh spring air and exotically clad ladies smoking Vogue cigarettes, and you're left with a bar cluttered with round tables which are too small to fit your drink on, miserable staff and food that no-one really wants. Let's face it – nice as it is, outdoor seating just ain't practical when it's pissing down.
Mon-Sun 9-11

Meal for two: £28 (Various pasta dishes)

Denim

4a Upper St. Martin's Lane, WC2
(020) 7497 0376
⊖ Leicester Sq

Denim is a two-tiered, rip-off factory resembling a bright red asylum cell. The lunatics that pose around it labour under the impression that yes they are important, and yes you do get what you pay for. Neither is true – although it gets filthily busy at the weekends both in the bar and the skanky-cool club downstairs, luke-warm drinks and over-inflated egos don't make for a good night out.
Mon-Sat 12-2, Sun 3.30-12.30

www.itchylondon.co.uk

Detroit

35 Earlham St, WC2
(020) 7240 2662 🚇 **Covent Garden**

You can tell this place thinks it's a bit cool, hidden away down Earlham St with obscure DJs and the kind of bar staff that have modelling contracts on the side. Lots of design-conscious lighting and sandy walls, but all in all, not a bad place. Just try and get the Flintstones theme out of your head...you'll see what we mean when you go.
Mon-Sat 5-12
Meal for two: £32 (Salmon)

Fuel

21 The Market, WC2 (020) 7836 2137
🚇 **Covent Garden**

Right in the centre of the piazza, beneath the covered market, Fuel is a maze of alcoves and tiny spaces. Cosy early evening for a bit of romance and reckless champagne buying. Tends to fill up later on with suits and marketing girls. Either a good or bad thing, depending on how scruffy and intolerant you're feeling.
Mon-Sat 10.30-2, Sun 10.30-11.30
Meal for two: £24 (Pizza)

The Langley

5 Langley St, WC2
(020) 7836 5005 🚇 **Covent Garden**

The Langley is a classy little number. Cool, minimal, lounge-style décor and handily dim lighting making everyone seem a damn sight sexier than they really are, and when that includes you, you really can't complain. Most importantly the Langley is fun. A line 'em up happy hour everyday from 5-7pm, music that induces a spontaneous boogie and a crowd that won't frown too heavily if you start moonwalking across the floor. Although the caterpillar is strictly out of the question.
Mon-Sat 4.30pm-1am, £3 after 10pm
Mon-Thu, £5 Fri-Sat
Meal for two: £36 (Roast rack of lamb)

La Perla

28 Maiden Lane, WC2
(020) 7240 7400 🚇 **Covent Garden**

'Tequila... it makes me happy'. Thanks for that Terrorvision, but no, it doesn't, more somewhat insane and a touch nauseous. Still, if you fancy propping the bar up and knocking back some of the hard stuff then La Perla is the place for you. Suitably noisy, smoky and atmospheric with an impressive display of dangerously translu-

www.itchylondon.co.uk

cent Mexican liquids. Everything you need for a night that you'll regret in the morning.
Mon-Sat 12-11, Sun 5-10.30
Meal for two: £28 (Swordfish)

Long Island Iced Tea Shop
1 Upper St Martin's Lane, WC2
(020) 7240 3734
⊖ **Leicester Sq**
Dark, dingy and sweaty. Music consists of chart hits, and 70s and 80s boogie inducers. Don't be fooled into thinking this will be any different if you attend on an R&B or Hip Hop night. It won't. An eclectic clientele of exuberant youths, Essex girls, Antipodean tourists and bizarrely, always a few well-to-do middle-aged men. All of them relishing in the opportunity of a night devoid of the necessity to dress with style, dance with finesse, or indeed act with any sophistication. In fact the only constant in the crowd is that everybody is absolutely, gob-dribblingly pissed. Despite the name of the place, the cocktails aren't as good as they could be and they have a habit of claiming that they don't do cocktails when the bar is busy. Pump monkeys.
Mon-Sat 12-3, Sun 12-10.30, Admission after 9 £3-10

Retox Bar
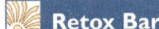
Corner Piazza/Russell St, WC2
(020) 7240 5330
⊖ **Covent Garden**
The crazy kids at Retox have hit upon a concept. Retox is the opposite of detox and involves a prescription of shots to up your toxin levels. Now call me stupid but this doesn't exactly strike as a novel phenomenon – surely bars have been retoxing for years, they just didn't feel the need to tell us? Whatever, this basement bar makes a nice change. More suited to a one-on-one chat than a group night out, primarily because the seating is minimal and quite uncomfortable. It looks good, but it's not relaxing. More drop in, drop your shots and drop out.
Mon-Wed 5-1, Thu-Sat 5-3, Admission Thu/Sat £5 after 9.30

Saint
8 Great Newport St, WC2
(020) 7240 1551 ⊖ **Leicester Sq**
Bar guides are always describing this place as stylish, purple and super cool and packed with more stars than the heavens. Stylish and purple maybe, but not a celebrity in sight and frankly, the most

www.itchylondon.co.uk

arsey door staff we've ever encountered. Full of people who really should have somewhere better to go.
Mon-Thu 5-2, Fri 5-3, Sat 7.30-3. Admission after 9pm Thu £5, Fri/Sat £7
Meal for two: £36 (Teriyaki salmon with tomato, baby spinach and noodles)

Spot

29 Maiden Lane, WC2
(020) 7379 5900 ⊖ **Covent Garden**
An odd place with unnecessarily high, clinical-looking bars, a tiled floor and a raised back room painted in a Sistine Chapel-esque style. Great for watching football too. The thing about Spot is that you know you're not 'where it's at', but who gives a toss when everyone's having a good time, concentrating on the drinking rather than who's wearing the latest Evisu twat range of denim.
Mon-Sun 12-1, Admission £5 Fri/Sat

Pubs

The Crown and Anchor
22 Neal St, WC2 (020) 7836 5649
⊖ **Covent Garden**
Lolling around somewhere in the murky area between a pub and style-bar. There's the obligatory pub-styled ground floor with sports screens and jukebox but a laughable lack of seating. Upstairs though, it looks like Lawrence Llewellyn Bowen has had a hand in designing some frankly cacky and painful plastic chairs, and some oh-so-trendy tables. Average.

Freedom Brewing Co

41 Earlham St, WC2
(020) 7240 0606 ⊖ **Covent Garden**
Blessedly free from tourists, this is your chance to organise a genuine piss-up in a brewery. Freedom is perfect for those lazy weekend afternoons that turn into evenings. Offering home-grown brews

and tasty bar snacks in a stylish, chilled and spacious basement. Get your ale sampling hat on.

The Nag's Head
10 James St, WC2 (020) 7836 4678
⊖ **Covent Garden**
If you are stood at the tube station a bit cold or dying of thirst then yes, the Nag's Head is the perfect option. Other than that there's no good reason to step inside. Unless average is your middle name and you fear a bit of excitement might kill you.

Princess Louise
208-209 High Holborn, WC1
(020) 7405 8816
⊖ **Holborn**
A truly spectacular Victorian pub with

THE INDEPENDENT The best writers, the sharpest opinions

elaborate décor. If you're anywhere in the vicinity it is your duty to visit. One of the best pubs in central London, you'll wonder why you ever bothered going anywhere else.

Punch and Judy

40 The Market, The Piazza, WC2
(020) 7379 0923
⊖ Covent Garden

This pub has one principal attraction – it's impressively positioned balcony overlooking Covent Garden's general hubbub. But when you inevitably tire of spitting on the heads of oblivious tourists and accept that it is not worth freezing your ass for the novelty of being outside, the appeal ends. Basically it's full of tourists and locals who cannot think of anywhere else to hold their reunions.

Restaurants

AKA

18 West Central St, WC1
(020) 7836 0110
⊖ Tottenham Court Rd

Mr C's annexe to The End (bar downstairs/restaurant above) is wickedly stylish. A definite place to be, and open late from Wednesday to Saturday. It feels like an old storage depot with a massive square bar, littered with chrome and glass tables and chairs. Always crowded with the young and cool, it's a definite top spot amongst central London's bar and restaurant scene.
Mon-Sat 6-3
Meal for two: £35 (Fennel and rosemary risotto)

Café Pacifico

5 Langley St, WC2 (020) 7379 7728
⊖ Covent Garden

Allegedly London's oldest Mexican restaurant and one of the most fun places to eat in the area. Challenge your mates to a chilli eating competition, down a load of tequila and try and snog the waiting staff. The food is great and properly hot – not one for wimps.
Mon-Sat 12-12, Sun 12-11
Meal for two: £28 (Burrito)

you've tried this one...now try them all 17 other cities to indulge in

covent garden

Food for Thought
31 Neal St, WC2 (020) 7836 9072
⊖ Covent Garden

Cheap as chips veggie cuisine. All a bit earthy and health conscious and at these prices, we're not complaining. Ideal when you're just plain hungry and don't want to shell out a small fortune to sit in the restaurant equivalent of the Design Museum. Lunch in Covent Garden sorted, but not the best place to take a hot date. Well, unless they're a die-hard vegetarian hippy type who likes their food 'thoughtful'.
Mon-Sat 9.30-20.30, Sun 12-4
Meal for two: £8 (Vegetable stir-fry, BYO)

The Ivy
1 West St, WC2 (020) 7836 4751
⊖ Leicester Sq

Celebrity engagements and record deals are celebrated here. But they need a certain amount of normal folk to make it worth the famous people's effort with their outfits. The waiting list for a table can run to a couple of months which doesn't make for a very spontaneous evening out, but it's not massively expensive, and well, frankly we haven't actually been, so who are we to comment? We know someone who has though, and they loved it. If you can't wait for one of your mates to hit the big time, get that table booked in advance.
Mon-Sun 12-3 then 5.30-12
Meal for two: £37 (Salmon fishcakes)

Joe Allen
13 Exeter St, WC2 (020) 7836 0651
⊖ Covent Garden

Tucked away in a side street off The Strand, Joe Allen is where the stars of the stage hang out and sip bourbons with their steak. The food is good and the largely French staff make you feel important. Still a place to be seen for those in the know after twenty-five years. Get down there before or after a show and you'll see what we mean.
Mon-Fri 12-12.45, Sat 11.30-12.45, Sun 11.30-11.30
Meal for two: £35 (Baked cod)

Hand book

www.itchylondon.co.uk

Tell us about yourself?
James, 18, Student, lives Palmer's Green
Student eh? Where d'you play your drinking games? Purple Turtle
And for a change from Pot Noodles?
Bar Gansa's food is top
Skiving lectures tommorrow?
Naturally. After a night at The End
You love London then?
Yeah, there's always loads going on

Livebait

21 Wellington St, WC2 (020) 7836 7161
⊖ Covent Garden
Handy place to pick up some grouting tips before you decorate your new bathroom. A veritable tile-arama. Food wise we're talking fish, shellfish and anything else you might find inhabiting your nearest ocean at, 'let's complain about the price of fish' prices. So basically, not cheap and full of classy thirty something types. The kind of people who actually like oysters and don't just eat them because they think it looks cool.
Mon-Sat 12-11.30
Meal for two: £40 (Five spiced tuna loin)

Souk

27 Litchfield St, WC2 (020) 7240 1796
⊖ Covent Garden
Experience North Africa in the heart of London with this fabulously authentic restaurant. Low seating, drapes and belly dancers. Seriously, cancel your flight to Marrakesh and stay put. With food this good and surroundings this opulent you really might as well.
Mon-Sun 12-12
Meal for two: £30 (Couscous)

Clubs

Browns

4 Great Queen St, WC2 (020) 7831 0802
⊖ Holborn
Quite why this place bothers to be a members club we'll never know. It's strictly B-list and hardly worth the bother. The prices rise as you ascend the stairs and if you make it into the VIP room at the top you may well be lucky enough to encounter someone who used to be a model, or a soap actor or starred in an advert for the Halifax or something. Downstairs is still too expensive to ever be fun and weighted heavily with knee-rubbing letches. And whatever you do, don't sit down as they'll force you to buy champers for the privilege. Truly annoying.

The End

18 West Central St, WC1 (020) 7419 9199
⊖ Tottenham Court Rd
Super-cool club, decent drinks prices and

RIZLA+ It's what you make of it.

covent garden

Can I click it..?

...Yes you can!

Low cost, high speed Internet access **24 hours** a day from just **£1**

easyEverything
the world's largest Internet cafés

Tottenham Court Road -Tube Exit 2 . Oxford Street - Opposite Bond Street Tube
Trafalgar Square - Opposite Charing X Station . Kensington High Street - Exit Tube, turn left
Victoria - Opposite BR Main Line Station

quality music. An all-round gem of a venue set in an old Post Office building. Industrial décor and fountains suit the mood and the entirely poser-free clientele, making for some serious good night out potential. The best thing about The End is that despite its size it retains an intimate feel. And Mr C's DJ mates can spin a tune or two. The best club in the area and one of the best in central London.

The Gardening Club
4 The Piazza, WC2 (020) 7497 3154
⊖ **Covent Garden**

Low ceilings, two bars, Playstations, a large film screen and a spacious dancefloor. However, except for the odd night, think trendy tourists alternating their night between here and The Rock Garden, which the club adjoins. Worth a look as it is a decent venue, but not guaranteed to make you come back for more.

The Rock Garden
6-7 The Piazza, WC2 (020) 7836 4052
⊖ **Covent Garden**

You know your mate Dave, the one who's in that band that nearly got signed? Well, apparently someone from Radio One loves them, and, well, they've got a new drummer and they're really good, honest, so hows about paying £4 to see them thrash around on a pokey stage at the Rock Garden this Wednesday? Oh yes please. That was the first and last time I will ever visit this hell-hole of a place. Hideous. The restaurant is packed with Americans harping on about themselves, wearing stupid hats and eating burgers. The club/bar is dingy, full of unfortunate looking people and the aforementioned bad bands that will never, ever make it (sorry Dave).

Stringfellow's Cabaret of Angels
16-19 Upper St Martin's Lane, WC2
(020) 7240 5534
⊖ **Leicester Sq**

A chance to turn those drunken evenings spent claiming to be a page three girl former ex of Stringy's into reality. Or, just a plain as you like opportunity to stare at naked flesh. Pete it seems has an eye for the ladies, and if his cabaret is anything to go by, a damned keen one at that. Beautiful girls, with an inability to keep their clothes on all set in stylish surroundings. Female-friendly, celeb-friendly and the best place to ogle semi-clad women without feeling like a dirty old man. Don't be shy.

leicester square & piccadilly

www.itchycity.co.uk

Not to be confused with Lie-Chester Square, which must be around here somewhere and inhabited by the entirety of the US of A. Leicester Square is plain as you like tacky. Full of freaks, tourists and the drunken offspring of high profile political figures. And Piccadilly? A toned down version of the above, getting classier as you go west towards Green Park.

Bars

10 Tokyo Joe's

85 Piccadilly, W1
(020) 7495 2595 ⊖ **Piccadilly Circus**
One of the rare breed of members' bars, actually worth blagging your way into. Tokyo Joe's is pure white minimal chic

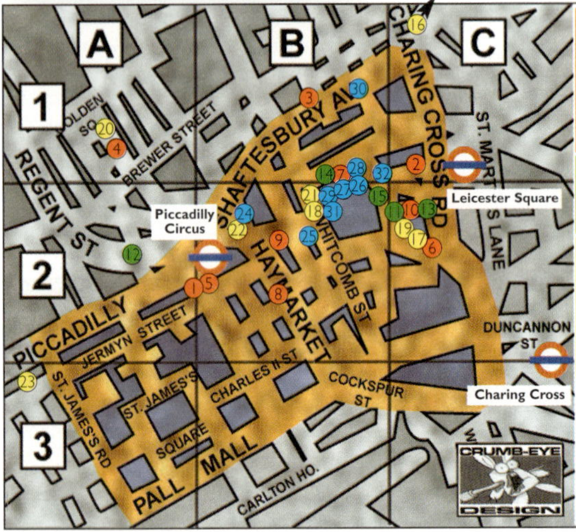

Bars
1. 10 Tokyo Joe's
2. Cork and Bottle
3. Curzon Soho Bar
4. Midas Touch
5. On Anon
6. Oxygen
7. Red Cube
8. Sports Café
9. Tiger Tiger
10. Zoo Bar

Pubs
11. Bear and Staff
12. Cheers
13. Faun & Firkin
14. Hogshead
15. Moon Under Water

Restaurants
16. Alfred Bar & Restaurant
17. Indian Akash
18. Manzi's
19. Mr Wu
20. Nine Golden Square
21. Poon's
22. Rainforest Café
23. The Ritz

Clubs
24. Bar Rumba
25. Café de Paris
26. Capital Club
27. Equinox
28. Hippodrome
29. Home
30. Limelight
31. Sound
32. Voodoo Lounge

with ever-changing ambient lighting. Not everyone in here's a millionaire and they do get drunk and flail round the dance floor like you should on a Friday night. Get that friend of a friend who knows the barman to put your name down.
Tue-Sat 5-4am Membership £300 a year

Cork and Bottle
44-46 Cranbourn St, WC2
(020) 7734 7807
⊖ **Leicester Sq**
Unusually classy bar for these parts, incongruously situated next to a sex-shop. The Cork and Bottle is a real find, especially for wine lovers. Not a drop of beer or a Barcardi Breezer in sight – just wall to wall wine. Situated in a basement it could easily go unnoticed but tuck in and be consumed in a world of civility. No dress code as such, but a classy establishment where you wouldn't want to turn up in your shellsuit.
Mon-Sat 11-12, Sun 12-10.30
Meal for two: £24 (Steak sandwich)

Curzon Soho Bar
93-107 Shaftesbury Ave, W1
(020) 7734 2255
⊖ **Piccadilly Circus**
A real discovery. The downstairs bar, open to members and cinema-goers, is spacious and chilled, offering sensibly priced drinks and bargain meals. Upstairs is perfect – when you just want a drink, a seat and no more hassle. Any night of the week. Don't tell everyone though – this is strictly between you and me.

Mon-Sun 12-11
Meal for two: £20 (Olives, humous and bread)

Midas Touch
4 Golden Square, W1
(020) 7287 9247 ⊖ **Piccadilly Circus**
You can't help but notice the amount of dingy pubs trying to re-invent themselves as stylish bars these days. At Midas Touch though, it's exactly the opposite. Its pubby interior tries desperately to be authentic old school, even flogging real ales. But, to the trained eye, it is without a doubt a yuppie bar. Stop trying to deny your breeding Midas Touch, admit it – you went to public school and your Dad owns Hertfordshire.
Mon-Sat 12-11
Meal for two: £24 (Sausage and mash)

On Anon
The London Pavillion,
Piccadilly Circus, W1 (020) 7287 8008
⊖ **Piccadilly Circus**
Motivating pissed-up mates to move on has never been easier. On Anon offers a

 Find places for late drinks on your WAP
wap.itchylondon.co.uk

leicester square & piccadilly   35

TOP FIVE... Cheap Eats

1. Wagamama (p15)
2. Food for Thought (p30)
3. La Porchetta (p56)
4. Pepper Tree (p86)
5. Curzon Soho Bar (p35)

staggering eight bars in one, meaning a mere stumble from New York loft to Canadian wood cabin. Hilarious make-shift décor but novel enough to make it wholeheartedly worth a visit. The booth bar adds a certain finesse, with stylish booths overlooking the mayhem of Piccadilly Circus – grab a date, a couple of cocktails and enjoy the view.
Mon-Sat 5-3 Admission Mon-Wed £3 after 11, Thu £5 after 10, Fri/Sat £10 after 10
Bar snacks from £3

Oxygen
17-18 Irving St, WC2
(020) 7930 0907 Leicester Sq
An inevitable tourist trap situated on the south side of Leicester Sq, Oxygen has three floors, with a dance floor in the basement and attempts to be dark and brooding. Together with cocktails, which are probably the best thing about the place, you can for a price, buy oxygen canisters to replenish your alcohol-depleted energy and give you a high. Complete bollocks. Don't waste your money and ultimately don't waste your time.
Mon-Wed 4-1, Thu 4-2, Fri-Sat 4-3, Sun 4-10.30
Oxygen: £8/£12

Red Cube
1 Leicester Place, WC2
(020) 7287 8050 Leicester Sq
From the makers of Sugar Reef, another over priced bar/restaurant frequented by pop kids and people with more money than sense. Opulent, glamorous and less in your face than it's Soho sister. Still, we can't bring ourselves to say it's worth the money. Sorry.
Mon-Sat 6-12 (Club open 'til 3am)
Admission £15 after 11
Meal for two: £57 (Roast cod)

Sports Café
80 Haymarket, SW1 (020) 7839 8300
Piccadilly Circus
A shrine to all things sport and one of the only places in central London where you can watch non-London teams. On account of the fact that this place has more screens than your average Dixon's, they can afford to be generous to visiting Leeds fans. They also offer pool tables, table football and a bizarre, basketball enclosure containing a mass of over-enthusiastic, whooping Americans. Take pleasure in calling them soft and complain loudly about how they have no idea what football is.
Mon-Thu 12-2, Fri-Sat 12-3, Sun 12-10.30

Tiger Tiger
29 Haymarket, SW1
(020) 7930 1885 Piccadilly Circus
A club, café, bar and restaurant all rolled into one. Fairly strict on its over twenty fives and smart dress code policies, helping to maintain a 'work off that executive

stress' image. Standing room only in the bar at weekends, but manages to capture that lucrative middle ground market – too old to go to a noisy club and too young for old men's boozers? This place hits the spot. Look out for the guy with the giddy responsibility of 'Property Control' who gets right narky should your bag encroach a few centimetres into the aisle. Easy tiger.
Mon-Sat 12-3, Sun 12-11.30. Admission Mon-Wed £3 after 11, Thu £5 after 10, Fri/Sat £8 after 10
Meal for two: £30 (Curried chicken)

Zoo Bar

13-18 Bear St, WC2
(020) 7839 4188 ⊖ **Leicester Sq**
If you aspire to the flashy, young professional with a taste by-pass school of thought, you'll be happy here. A meat-market at weekends where cash is flashed in the hope of a pull. And once the happy hour (1-7) cocktail novelty has worn off there's not a right lot to keep you here. The basement club, Venom is unadulterated tack and to continue the theme, laydees get in free on Thursday nights. A trail of sad, lonely, and unlikely to be anything other than single men are right behind them. Rumour has it that a new VIP lounge has just opened on the top floor – somewhere for Ian Beale to get the long overdue adulation he deserves then.
Mon-Sat 1-2.30 (club opens 'til 3.30) Admission Fri/Sat £5 after 9, £8 after 10

Pubs

Bear & Staff
11 Bear St, WC2
⊖ **Leicester Sq**
A better and less predictable and more traditional choice than the Firkin. There's no escaping the Leicester Square night-mare scenario, but as choices in the area go it's not a bad one.

Cheers
72 Regent St, W1 (020) 7494 3322
⊖ **Piccadilly Circus**
Sometimes, you just want to go where everybody knows your name. And at those times this would be a fairly bad choice. Vaguely similar to the US comedy bar, but packed to the rafters with tourists and shoppers seeking refuge from Regent St. Pretty good for watching sport or cocktails, but a friendly local with a laugh a minute, it ain't.
Mon-Sat 12-3, Sun 12-10.30. Food served until 11. Happy hour 3-8.
Meal for two: £26 (Any of Norm's burgers)

Faun & Firkin

18 Bear St, WC2
Leicester Sq

Smaller than your average Firkin, which actually works to make it even more unbearable than usual. Not bad, if you just want a pint and you can't be bothered to look further afield. But any other day, it's just too crowded and depressing to be worth setting foot in.

Hogshead

5 Lisle St, WC2 (020) 7437 3335
Leicester Sq

Yet another chain of pubs intent on re-creating 'ye-olde-ale-houses' in a city where style bars and cocaine rule. Spacious with two floors and a big no smoking section for those who haven't yet realised that smoking's cool. Often surprisingly empty for such a bustling location. However, with great deals on food, this is your answer for a cheap night out with a mate.

Moon Under Water

28 Leicester Sq, WC2
(020) 7839 2837 **Leicester Sq**

Cheaper than cheap. And if that's your priority, the perfect choice for a few select beverages.

Restaurants/Restaurant Bars

Alfred Bar and Restaurant

245 Shaftesbury Avenue WC2
(020) 7240 2566
Leicester Sq

Appealing and classy both outside and in, and strictly no smoking. The menu is diverse and extravagant, featuring the likes of shark and haggis. The wine list is long and complicated, but seeing as we both know you're going to order the house white, it's hardly a problem.
Mon-Fri 12-3.30pm then 6-11, Sat 6-11
Meal for two: £40 (Crispy belly of pork)

Indian Akash Restaurant

14-15 Irving St, WC2 (020) 7930 0744
Leicester Sq

Leicester Square not worked it's magic on you? Looking for a way to make the most out of a bad night? Then get thee to Akash. With last orders at 11.45 you can rectify the situation with food, and if you like, more drink. Licensed until midnight.
Mon-Sun 12-12
Meal for two: £22 (Chicken korma)

Manzi's

1-2 Leicester St, WC2 (020) 7734 0224
Leicester Sq

Johan Strauss once lodged in what is now Manzis. Whether he would have

enjoyed the grating French music piped out to the tourists as they tuck into their French cuisine is questionable. However, I'm sure he would've appreciated the huge range of fresh seafood on offer, and the surprisingly pleasant staff.
Mon 12-3 then 5.30-11.45, Tue-Sat 12-11.45, Sun 6-10.45
Meal for two: £35 (Seafood platter for two)

Mr Wu

6-7 Irving St, WC2 (020) 7839 6669
Leicester Sq
Offers some amazing multi-course banquets at bargain basement prices. No glitz, no glamour but renowned amongst Chinese-loving cheapskates.
Mon-Sun 12-11.30
Meal for two: £20 (10 course buffet £4.50)

Nine Golden Square

9 Golden Sq, W1 (020) 7439 2424
Piccadilly Circus
Trendy, basement restaurant offering posh nosh and palm trees. Cool décor, ad execs (M & C Saatchi are just across the road) and high prices. The bar makes a good place to hang out pre or post dinner and talk about your latest campaign. Super-comfy chairs and tropical plants – like being in a conservatory.
Mon-Wed 12-3 then 5-10.30, Thu-Fri 12-3 then 5-11
Meal for two: £38 (Pan-fried sole fillets, saffron cream, potato puree and tomato)

Chinatown

London's Chinatown is focused round Gerrard St and holds all the overpriced Oriental delights you'd expect. Specialist supermarkets, gift shops and ornate street furniture. There are some gems amongst the tourist traps and for post piss-up food it can't be beaten. Some of our favourites are **Poons** (see review), Gerrard's Corner (30 Wardour St, 020 7437 0984) and the **Aroma** restaurants (Gerrard St/Shaftesbury Ave, 020 7439 2720/ 020 7437 0377). Well worth checking out. Watch out for massages without the extras on Sundays.

Poon's

4 Leicester St, WC2 (020) 7437 1528
Leicester Sq
Quality Chinese just at the entrance of Chinatown. Staff can be a bit unfriendly but not so hostile as to warrant no tip at all. Recently refurbished with a relaxing atmosphere, great for dining with the love of your life. Check out the diced ostrich if you're feeling adventurous.
Mon-Sun 12-12
Meal for two: £25 (Set menu for two)

Rainforest Café

20 Shaftesbury Ave, WC2 (020) 7434 3111
Leicester Sq
A crystal clear waterfall trickles into the small lagoon below, parrots and a vicious looking anaconda stare down from the ceiling as you tuck into your volcanic cob

salad, and you just can't help but wonder if this theme restaurant has taken things a touch too far. It's not that the food is bad, it's just disconcerting being surrounded by plastic chimps as you tuck into your barbecued ribs (sorry, Mojo bones)?
Mon-Fri 12-10, Sat 11.30-7.45, Sun 11.30-10
Meal for two: £32 (Wallaby's Wok)

The Ritz

Ritz Hotel, Piccadilly, W1 (020) 7493 8181
Green Park

It's bloody expensive! (Well duh). Nevertheless quite simply the best tea, cucumber sandwiches, scones and delicate pastries in town. To be perfectly honest, if you're paying this much for tea, you should really make the most and cause utmost havoc by swearing loudly and throwing tantrums because your Earl Grey isn't regal enough. Beware there's a six week waiting list just to get a table and whatever you're wearing won't be acceptable.
Mon-Sat 11.30-11, Sun 12-10.30
Tea sittings 3.30 and 5, £27 per person

Clubs

Bar Rumba

36 Shaftesbury Ave, W1
(020) 7287 6933
Piccadilly Circus

Given its central location and worse than that, dangerous proximity to the Trocadero, you may find it hard to believe that this place has any redeeming qualities. It has. Honest. Every night of the week is buzzing with a mix of Latino, funk and jazz and a happy crowd with a larger than average contingent of proper Londoners. Bar Rumba is a long running success story. Get down and get down.
Mon-Thu 5-3.30, Fri 5-4, Sat 7-6, Sun 8-2 Admission after 9, Mon £4, Tue-Thu £3, Fri-Sat £6. After 11, Wed-Thu £5, Fri-Sat £10. After midnight Sat £12.

Café de Paris

3 Coventry St, W1 (020) 7734 7700
Leicester Sq

Café de Paris plays host to some amazing events; album launches, fashion shows and premiere parties. And the ornate, old ballroom venue is the perfect setting for glamour, air kissing and networking. Thing is, all this high profile, posh stuff, attracts a certain type. Welcome to wannabe world. Men in suits, swigging Champagne and swearing blind they're mates with Jamie Theakston and girls in hot-pants and lip gloss pouting by the bar. The music may well be decent and the surroundings enticing, but the place is packed, expen-

Take a leaf out of our book

sive and has so many rules about where you can and can't stand/walk/breathe you'll be instantly confused. Like gate crashing an Eton school reunion mixed with a rugby scrum. By no means a bad choice for a night out – with a strong sense of irony, fake business cards and an unlimited overdraft facility, you'll have a great time.

Capital Club

Leicester Square, WC2 (020) 7434 0993
🚇 **Leicester Sq**

There's often a strange bloke wandering around Leicester Square with a sandwich board to promote this dire venue. You can tell all he wants is one person to say 'yes, OK give us a flyer and I'll come along later' – the poor guy is clearly on the edge. Be warned, like your good selves we're sympathetic to his cause. But frankly, we would rather see him perish than accept an invitation into this garage loving, Hooch-drinking, Silk Cut Extra Low-smoking pit of slagdom. If you're reading this, Mr strange bloke, we're sorry, but your gaff sucks. It's harsh but fair.

Hippodrome/Equinox

I Cranbour St (020) 6437 4311
Leicester Sq (020) 7437 1446
🚇 **Leicester Sq**

Achtung! Attention! Cuidado! Ernstz, Claude, Gustavo, what are you doing? Can't you see? Are you going to follow those other gormless rucksack-wearing lemmings into these universally shameful dens of tourist-fleecing despair? Are you drawn by the tacky euro beats? Or the glamour of caged dancers? Is it the billows of dry ice that presses your buttons? Look, go if you have to – just don't return home saying you've lived it large in London.

Home

I Leicester Sq, WC2 (020) 7909 1111
🚇 **Leicester Sq**

Two years ago the Home and Fabric propaganda machines were stirring up talk of the return of the super club to the South (if you've ever visited the Hacienda you know what we mean) and the race was on to open first. Home may have won that race, but in terms of kudos, it was always a non-starter, located in very un-cool Leicester Square to Fabric's cooler than thou Farringdon. As it turns out the two clubs play to entirely different clubbing audiences. Home is strictly for funky beat lovers, bringing true northern spirit to London. We're talking real McCoy Graham Park-esque garage – *you know*, as evolved from 1980s US club The Garage: soulful, vocal, uplifting, with a dubby baseline. And with a fantastic venue to boot – what the original Home did for Sydney, this one's doing for London. A clubland must visit.

Sound

**Swiss Centre, Leicester Sq, W1
(020) 7863 7312
↔ Leicester Sq**

Bar, club, restaurant, you know the sort. Sound is great for pre-club drinks and hosts some mighty fine nights of its own, most notably the flares and afro-tastic Carwash. Top cocktails, smooth service and maximum fun factor, but smack bang in the heart of Leicester Square so not the most salubrious clientele. Who cares – it's a good laugh, and one with celebrity spotting potential – the Pepsi Chart Show is filmed upstairs.
Mon-Wed 5-12, Thu-Sat 5-4

Limelight

**136 Shaftesbury Ave, W1 (020) 7434 0572
↔ Leicester Sq**

"Pleez be geevin me one of your lager beers" overheard at the bar, which kind of sums the place up. This ex-Presbyterian chapel offers five function rooms, catering for different music tastes – handy as long as your taste ranges from averagely OK to dire. From commercial house to 80s nights, we're talking cheesy but tourist-infested and heaving, so they must be doing something right. Beware lecherous men hanging around the bar and gold-digging, young at heart laydees hanging around the men's. Over 20s only.

Voodoo Lounge

**7-9 Cranbourn St, W1 (020) 7287 7773
↔ Leicester Sq**

Pricey but appealing rock 'n' roll multi-level drinking den. The door staff are scary and you won't get any change from a tenner for a couple of drinks, but it's still entertaining. Wednesday's 'The Night of a Thousand Drums' is an intriguing, come along and have a go, interactive drumming session. Blimey, whatever next?

RIZLA+ www.rizla.com

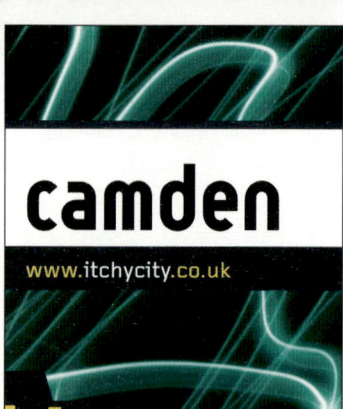

camden

www.itchycity.co.uk

Students, musos, Goths and rockers. Stepping outside Camden Town tube, you can't fail to notice the parading freak-show of stereotypes. This is what makes Camden cool. Relaxed, grungy and the only place in town for up and coming pop stars to start spreading their wings. There's no room for posers in NW1.

Bars

Bar Gansa

2 Inverness St, NW1
(020) 7267 8909 ⊖ **Camden Town**
Inverness Street's Spanish offering serves up tasty tapas and traditional Spanish dishes with a selection of regional riojas and local cervezas. It remains a firm

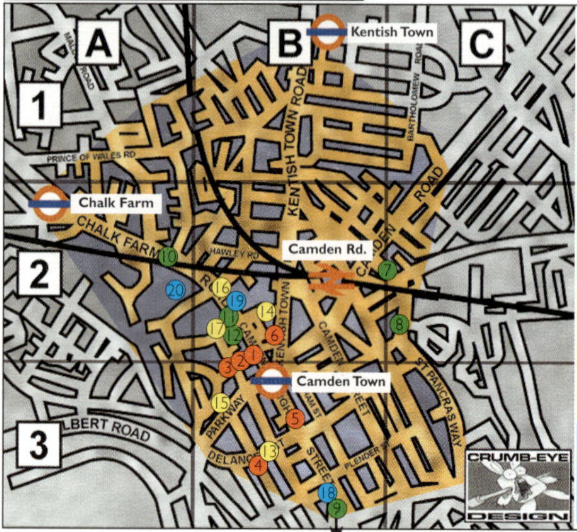

Bars
1. Bar Gansa
2. Bar Solo/Under Solo
3. Bar Vinyl
4. Martini's
5. The Oh Bar
6. WKD

Pubs
7. The Camden Brewing Co.
8. The Constitution
9. The Edinboro' Castle
10. The Monarch
11. The Oxford Arms
12. The World's End

Restaurants
13. Café Delancey
14. Mango Rooms
15. George & Niki's
16. Sauce barorganicdiner
17. Pie2Mash

Clubs
18. Camden Palace
19. The Electric Ballroom
20. HQs

www.itchylondon.co.uk

favourite, intimate and low-lit with a romantic edge. Gets crowded from Thursday to Sunday but if you want a drink after eleven, Gansa is definitely where it's at.
Mon-Wed 10-12, Thu-Sat 10-1, Sun 10-11
Meal for two: £20 (tapas)

Bar Solo/Under Solo
20 Inverness St, NW1 (020) 7482 4611
⊖ **Camden Town**
The most recent of the trendy Inverness Street bars, looks and feels like a lush Moroccan harem with tented ceilings, wooden floors, and red velvet sofas. Purchase a beer, find your corner, pop a cigar between your lips and you become the sultan. Oh alright, you don't, but late

opening and a young crowd make this a consistently good choice.
Mon-Sun 9-1
Meal for two: £28 (Seafood platter)

Bar Vinyl
6 Inverness St, NW1 (020) 7681 7898
⊖ **Camden Town**
Small, laid back and very hip, Bar Vinyl (above Vinyl Addiction), has a homely, homeboy feel. Decks, a graffiti mural (perhaps to distract customers from the informative writing in the ladies) and hoards of attractive DJ wannabes and their hangers on. A fun place to chill out,

check out the talent and hone your scratching skills at their regular jamming sessions.
Mon-Thu 11-11, Fri-Sat 11-12, Sun 12-10.30

Martini's
7 Delancey Street, NW1 (020) 7387 7008
⊖ **Camden Town**
Very suave and sophisticated, Martini's is trying to cater for something Camden neither wants nor needs, it would be better suited to New York in the eighties. Martini cocktails, champagne on ice and

jazz on the stereo – it does have a certain kitsch appeal. Somewhere you imagine the local indie kids should be celebrating their record deals, but it seems they don't. A lovely place that just doesn't fit its location.
Tue-Sat 5-11

The Oh Bar
111-113 Camden High St, NW1
(020) 7383 0667
⊖ Camden Town

Previously just the O-Bar, and presumably re-named for all the punters who walked in and said, "Oh – it's not that bad". Which it isn't. It's not going to end up being your favourite haunt in the world – but it's good for a laugh and end of the evening vodka casualties are by no means treated with disdain.
Mon-Sat 12-11, Sun 12-10.30 (recently lost late licence but watch this space)
Meal for two: £24 (Various thai dishes)

WKD
18 Kentish Town Road, NW1
(020) 7267 1869
⊖ Camden Town

This dark but colourful bar/club is populated by an up for it twenty something crowd, making for a lively, raucous atmosphere. It is also renowned for its ability to attract scantily clad and attractive females. Not that a little thing like that would sway you. The weekend music policy is based on the rarest of grooves – which is their way of describing 70s and 80s disco classics, and the door policy is strictly laid back. Add to this some of the most entertaining bar staff this side of the river and you're onto a winner.
Mon-Wed 12-2, Thu 12-2.30, Fri-Sat 12-3, Sun 12-1 Admission £3-7 after 10
Meal for two: £22 (Thai green curry)

TOP FIVE...
Pulling – not fussy
1. **Strawberry Moons** (p16)
2. **Zoo** (p37)
3. **Crazy Larry's** (p95)
4. **WKD** (p46)
5. **Clapham Grand** (p87)

Pubs

The Camden Brewing Company
1 Randolph St, NW1 (020) 7267 9829
⊖ Camden Town/Camden Rd rail

Smoking dwarves beware – you won't like this pub – the cigarette machine is virtually on the ceiling. Everyone else will absolutely love it. They don't actually do much brewing, but they do provide great sofas, cool tunes, funky mirrors, a mysterious spiral staircase and roaring log fires on a winter's day. Without a doubt, this is the best pub in Camden.
Mon-Thu 12-11, Fri-Sat 12-12, Sun 12-11

The Constitution

42 St Pancras Way, NW1 (020) 7387 4805
⊖ Camden Town

Every drinker has certain inalienable rights: The right to a decent pint; access to a pool table; a quiz machine; a jukebox and Sky TV. All in a classic pub atmosphere, with the amendment of a terrace overlooking the canal if you get sick of the guy with the beard putting on too much Level 42. You should go — it's in The Constitution.

The Edinboro' Castle

57 Mornington Cres, NW1 (020) 7255 9651
⊖ Camden Town/Mornington Cres

The Edinboro' Castle has a polished finish. A huge, high ceilinged, open pub which is trendy without being threatening. Not the best place for getting hammered with the lads, the lights are far too bright for bad behaviour. It is however a genuinely nice pub, perfect for obscure conversations and getting slowly drunk.

Monarch

49 Chalk Farm Rd, NW1
(020) 7916 1049
⊖ Camden Town/Chalk Farm

Plays host to Barfly, promoters of up and coming bands, meaning live music every night. And as gig pubs go, this one is surprisingly pleasant. Get the lagers in and try and spot the next Travis — or have a game of table football and wait for the next lot if you've been lumbered with the next Menswear.
Mon-Thu 8-12, Fri-Sat 8-2 Admission Fri/Sat £5

The Oxford Arms

265 Camden High St, NW1
(020) 7267 4945
⊖ Camden Town

Open 'til midnight, which some would say is at least an hour too long.
Mon-Thu 11-12, Fri-Sat 11-1, Sun 11-10.30 Admission £2 after 10.30

The World's End

174 Camden High St, NW1
(020) 7482 1932 ⊖ Camden Town

'Probably the biggest pub in the world' boasts this boozer — which is great, if you think that quantity is more important than quality — in which case you'll be delighted with the cavernous, soulless acres of drinking room available. This pub's only function is as a place to meet people, before you go and find somewhere good. The World's End? You'll think it is.

Restaurants

Café Delancey

3 Delancey St, Camden, NW1
(020) 7387 1985 ⊖ Camden Town

In a romantic mood? Well, this makes a fine choice for an intimate meal for two. A candlelit, French Swiss restaurant with

quality food and excellent service. We're talking Frank Sinatra, classy décor and more than a touch of glamour. Being the kind of place that inspires sedate behaviour and decidedly non-raised voices, it wouldn't be a bad place to break up with someone either.
Mon-Sat 9-11.30, Sun 9-10
Meal for two: £30 (Salmon fish cakes)

Mango Rooms
10 Kentish Town Road, NW1
(020) 7482 5065
 Camden Town

Chilled out Caribbean restaurant with loads of atmosphere. Bright, cheery décor, reggae and great food. A modern take on all your Caribbean classics, so red snapper, ackee, plantain and curried goat, immaculately presented and totally delicious. It's also a cracking place during the week to just hang out with a few drinks. Worth the trip to Camden if you don't live in the area, and undoubtedly already a firm favourite if you do.
Mon 6-12, Tue-Sun 12-3 then 6-12
Meal for two: £30 (Ackee)

George & Niki's: The Golden Grill
38 Parkway, NW1 (020) 7485 7432
 Camden Town

George and Niki's is a well-kept secret; as near to a proper northern caff as you'll get in the south of England. You can order a fry up breakfast until 6pm, (2pm on Sundays) and the rest of the menu is typically British: roasts, fish and chips and spotted dick. The locals love it and television's highest paid stars have all dined here, Nick Kamen, Des Lynam, Anthea Turner, they've got 'photos to prove it. Last but not least, you get multi-coloured lollipops on your way out. If that's not reason enough to get yourself down here, then you've obviously never been to the Little Chef.
Mon-Sun 12-12
Meal for two: £19 (All day breakfast – we've assumed you'll want wine with that)

Sauce barorganicdiner
214 Camden High St, NW1
(020) 7482 0777
 Camden Town

Apparently organic doesn't have to mean freakishly healthy and wholesome, but

Roll up

invariably it does. Here you'll find simple, well-prepared food at reasonable prices. A fantastic range for vegetarians and a warm glow inside as you leave knowing that because of you, for one night only, the environment is safe from harm. Now remember that next time you're in Sainsbury's.

Mon-Sat 12-11, Sun 12-4.30

Meal for two: £22 (Veggie burger)

Pie2Mash

9-11 Jamestown Rd, NW1 (020) 7482 2770
 Camden Town

Pies and mash in a classy setting? It'll never work. Well, it seems it does. Perfect hangover food in a restaurant as far removed from greasy spoon as you can get. A definite weekend lunch essential. Lovely.

Mon-Sun 11-12

Meal for two: £28 (Sausage and mash)

Clubs

Camden Palace

**1a Camden High St, NW1
(020) 7387 0428**
 Camden Town

A massive venue, low on glamour but high on popularity, with the local student contingent anyway. Any night of the week you'll find varying levels of tacky chart hits and house anthems. Not somewhere we'd leap to recommend, but a good cheap night out, if the rest of your mates are up for it.

The Electric Ballroom

**184 Camden High Street, NW1
(020) 7485 9006**
 Camden Town

The Electric Ballroom is a huge, studenty, but not teenie bopper venue, where getting served, even on a Saturday night, isn't too much of a chore. The bouncers are happy to let entirely inappropriate crowds wander into the scariest Goth nights you've ever seen, though the Saturday disco-fests are for just about anyone. Electric Ballroom is a good old-fashioned, entertaining night out with prices to match. Let's face it, you'll have no problem pulling.

HQs

**West Yard, Camden Lock, NW1
(020) 7485 6044** **Camden Town**

Loft-style space above the lock: café by day, club space by night. Different promoters keep HQs buzzing, but varied over the weekends, with Paul 'Trouble' Anderson's famous uplifting garage nights and a general disco/funk kind of night on Saturday. It's a comfortable, no pretensions, anything goes kind of place. The crowd is casual and all the punters' good looking.

RIZLA+ It's what you make of it.

islington

www.itchycity.co.uk

Everyone in Islington should be a 20-stone, alcoholic given the ridiculous concentration of bars and restaurants along Upper St and Essex Rd. Fortunately, however, they are not. More a mix of posh families, Essex boys done good, champagne socialists and a handful of dodgy geezers.

Bars

25 Canonbury Lane

25 Canonbury Lane, N1
 Highbury & Islington

My, my, aren't we popular – everyone's talking about 25 Canonbury Lane. Well, if you count Time Out and the Evening Standard as everyone, and it seems quite a lot of people do. New on the scene

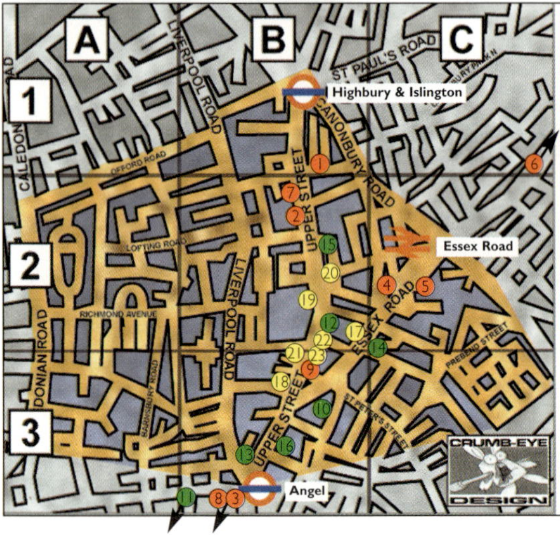

Bars
1. 25 Canonbury Lane
2. Bierodrome
3. Elbow Room
4. Embassy
5. Ice House
6. Lighthouse
7. Medicine Bar
8. Salmon & Compasses
9. Santa fe

Pubs
10. Camden Head
11. Filthy McNastys
12. King's Head Theatre
13. The Nag's Head
14. Old Queen's Head
15. The Royal Mail
16. The York

Restaurants
17. Bar & Dining House Islington
18. Cuba Libre
19. Granita
20. La Porchetta
21. Schnecke
22. Strada
23. Upper Street Fish Shop

and we're betting here to stay, offering cocktails, draught beers and damned good tapas. Make it your own before one journalist too many declares it the height of Islington hip.
Mon 5-11, Tue-Sat 12-11, Sun 12-10.30

Bierodrome
173-174 Upper St, N1
(020) 7226 5835
🚇 **Angel/Highbury & Islington**

An upmarket chain, with a trainspotter worthy array of Belgian beers. Stylish and surprisingly un-up-itself, with super-efficient staff – something of a novelty in this 'the customer is always wrong' city. You could describe the interior as log cabin meets Swedish sauna, but (and fairly inexplicably) I couldn't quite shake the feeling I was swigging my Leffe in an aircraft hanger. Bar snacks sound good, but are ridiculously small portioned. A beer lover's paradise – so, if you're sick of girly cocktails and nothing being on draught, get yourself down here and get shit-faced.
Mon-Sat 12-12, Sun 12-10.30
Meal for two: £25 (Belgo mussel pot with frites)

Elbow Room
89-91 Chapel Market, N1
(020) 7278 3244
🚇 **Angel**

Purple pool tables, 'it's your turn, hustler' vibrating pagers and a one-way mirror allowing girls to observe the, well, nothing that goes on in the boys toilets. The Elbow Room is cool without being intimidating and lends itself to serious drinking and overly flirtatious dancing. Everyone leaves with a tale to tell, or at the very least a fake mobile number. The queues can get a bit problematic at the weekend, so turn up early. If however, you do find yourself arriving late, this is one place worth standing in line for.
Mon-Wed 12-2, Thu-Sat 12-3, Sun 12-11. Admission Fri/Sat £2 after 9pm, £5 after 10pm
Meal for two: £23 (Cheeseburger)

Embassy
119 Essex Rd, N1
(020) 7226 9849 🚇 **Angel**

Dark lighting hides a multitude of furnishing sins, but the sordid, dark-orange glow emitted from wall lights creates a

THE INDEPENDENT ON SUNDAY — The best coverage of news & sport

islington 51

uniquely relaxed and intimate atmosphere. Or maybe it just seems that way because it's minuscule? Big fashion egos are kept at bay with the leftover furnishings of what looks like an old working men's club. Secluded corners are ideal for skiving off work or pretending you're famous. Definitely worth checking out their Sunday offerings when minor pop personalities, old and new, spin a few tunes for the crowd.
Mon-Thu 5-11, Fri-Sat 5-1, Sun 3-10.30

Ice House
142 Essex Road, N1 (020) 7359 2661
Angel
It's all a bit last days of disco in this small, newly established Islington bar. Now, don't take this as a reflection on the amount I can think of to say, but this place has amazingly good one2one reception. I jest you not, it's perfect, and the likes of Vodafone? Nothing! Other than that (which frankly is enough for me), this is a great place for serious debauchery, they won't tell you off for dancing on the bar, thou' you'd have to be a dwarf to attempt it and downing absinthe is de rigueur.
Mon-Thu 5-11, Fri-Sat 5-late, Sun 5-10.30

Lighthouse
382 Essex Rd, N1 (020) 7288 0685
Angel/Essex Rd rail
Ice House's older, less stylised, but more popular cousin. Dodgy décor, oversized lampshades, Elvis murals and a bubble machine. Shabby-chic bar hidden far enough down Essex Rd for your mates to sort out a night DJ'ing without forcing the rest of Islington's drinkers to endure their experimental tunes. You can hire the place out for the night for free with a Billy no-mates guarantee – if you don't fill the place then they'll throw open the doors and let some randoms in to make up the numbers.
Mon-Thu 5-11, Fri-Sat 5-late, Sun 5-10.30

Medicine Bar

181 Upper St, N1
(020) 7704 9536
Angel/Highbury & Islington
Dark, cool hangout at the top end of Upper St, set for refurbishment by early 2001. The music's always spot-on and the lighting's dim enough to have you convinced you're the hottest thing in town. The downside to this place is its seriously irritating door policy. They run a free membership system and operate this with militant force at weekends – heaven

forbid you should just wander past and think it looks like a decent place for a drink. No, no you've got to be in the know to hang-out here, which seems to suit its trendy clientele just fine.
Mon-Thu 4-12, Fri-Sat 12-1, Sun 12-10.30

Salmon & Compasses
58 Penton St, N1 (020) 7837 3891
Angel

In pre-Elbow Room days this was practically the only after-hours establishment in Angel, and apart from a pool table, there the similarity ends. Those lucky enough to have survived a night in Salmon & Compasses know it's hard to beat. The cool factor here is tongue-in-cheek, epitomised by an incongruous mix of cult tunes and cheesy pop from a turntable hovering above the bar – God is a precariously balanced DJ here. You come to pull, get pissed, throw up and rejoice in the fact that posing is not an option. Elbow Rooms may be the place of the moment but I have faith in Salmon & Compasses, its rotating disco ball and one and only pool table, after all, next year, pool will be out and dancing back in.
Mon-Wed 5-12, Thu-Fri 5-2, Sat 2-2, Sun 2-10.30. Admission Fri/Sat £3 after 9.30

Santa fe
75 Upper St, N1 (020) 7288 2288
Angel

Terracotta and orange = Mexico? Actually, Santa fe takes its inspiration from over the border in the US of A, and what they're doing here is New Mexico don't you know, and that's not to be confused with Tex Mex. Whatever, it's doing it well, helped along by the friendliest staff in London. Tip one, bypass the jeans and suit jacket combos posing at the bar and head straight for the long tables, great for groups and unnecessary loudness. Tip two, first time toilet trips are best made sober, blokes will think they're standing on the Las Vegas interstate and girls find themselves faced with barbed wire toilet seats. All a bit scary.
Mon-Sat 12-11, Sun 12-10.30
Meal for two: £28 (Green chilli burger)

Pubs

Camden Head
2 Camden Walk, N1 (020) 7359 0851
Angel

Traditional pub with a novel and locally renowned weekend comedy club. Satellite TV, fruit machines, pool tables, a

you've tried this one...now try them all **17 other cities to indulge in**

islington

beer garden and decent pub grub – what more could you ask for? A proper pub, with a proper North London crowd, so expect in jokes and local antique trade gossip. Handy if you're in the market for an old vase or two.

Filthy McNastys

68 Amwell St, EC1 (020) 7837 6067
Angel

Owned by members of the Pogues, Filthy's is a true Irish pub, from the sterling Guinness right down to the juke box. The kind of place you wished you'd known about earlier, with a full-on, up-for-it atmosphere seven days a week. Adorned with truly eclectic authentic memorabilia; the kind that other pubs can't even begin to compete with, and punters that don't bat an eyelid to passing celebrities. This place is the main reason Shane McGowan's always pissed.

Kings Head Theatre

115 Upper St, N1 (020) 7226 0364
Angel

Bizarre pub below the Kings Head Theatre. Old show posters and a shabby, bohemian/eccentric feel. Attracts an older, more sensible crowd, the kind of people who know endless, unnecessary facts about bygone stage stars and think that Puff Daddy is an insult.

The Nag's Head

12 Upper St, N1 (020) 7226 3756
Angel

Just across the road from The York and an arguably, nicer place to support your team. Decide for yourself; it's not exactly a Mods v Rockers style contention, just two pubs with tellies that happen to be near each other.

Old Queen's Head

44 Essex Rd, N1 (020) 7354 9273
Angel

A contradiction of a place. A spacious pub that feels a bit like a bar. A student feel but no overheard whinging about the horrific stress of four lectures a week. A good place for a casual get together or a full-on piss up. In fact, a good all-rounder, a decent pint and not a chrome light-fitting in sight.

TOP FIVE...
Watch the footie
1. The Spot (p28)
2. Fulhum Tup (p90)
3. The York (p55)
4. Sports Cafe (p36)
5. Shoeless Joe's (p103)

THE INDEPENDENT — The best coverage of news & sport

www.itchylondon.co.uk

The Royal Mail

153 Upper St, N1
Angel

When only a genuine boozer will do, this big, old-fashioned pub goes down a treat with the nearby sorting office workers. You know they work funny hours. Well, they always drink funny ones too... time to start making friends. No pretensions, just like pubs were meant to be.

The York

82 Islington High St, N1
(020) 7278 2095 Angel

Football mania. If sport scares you then the York is best avoided. A slave to its big screen TV, earning maximum respect from Islington's sport fans, but beware the colour of your shirt as this is an Arsenal area, and they won't give Welsh Man U fans the 'respect' they deserve. It does get packed, so don't expect a seat or a stress-free trip to the bar. Do, however, expect a buzzing atmosphere and raucous chanting.

Restaurants/Restaurant Bars

Bar & Dining House Islington

2 Essex Rd, N1 (020) 7704 8789
Angel

Back in the seventies, décor was brown, ten years later and you'd have bet the last page in your Filofax that black ash was here to stay... and now beige is cool again. Fickle indeed. A mere six months old and this classy restaurant serving modern

And you are?
Ed, 25, Musician, lives Clapham
Unemployed then. I suppose you want me to buy the drinks?
Always. At the Brixtonian Havana Club
Free for dinner? Maybe. Wagamama's?
And to show off your moves?
Straight to the Notting Hill Arts Club
Why London? And why not?
The tube on both counts. Intolerable

British food is already a firm favourite. More fitting for a sophisticated rendezvous with an attractive date than getting lagered with your work-mates. However, come the weekend the downstairs bar offers a more fitting atmosphere for the latter – scarily low ceilings, but you soon get used to feeling like a basketball player. Shoot some pool and enjoy the live music.

Mon-Wed 5-11, Thu-Sat 5-2, Sun 12-11
Meal for two: £30 (Swordfish)

Cuba Libre

72 Upper St, N1 (020) 7354 9998
Angel

The stuff office parties are made of. Tacky venue, good, authentic food and all hell

breaking loose in the bar after dinner. Not one for classy types or posers. This place is for getting wasted, swinging your hips and getting escorted from the premises at closing because you've forgotten that whole one-foot-in-front-of-the-other concept. A damned good laugh, though suffice to say there's only so many times you can listen to the Gypsy Kings.
Mon-Thu 11-11, Fri-Sat 11-2, Sun 11-10.30
Meal for two: £32 (Ropa-vieja, a Cuban dish of shredded beef)

Granita
127 Upper St, N1 (020) 7226 3222
Angel/Highbury & Islington
Far too posh and minimal to be fun, but serves up excellent Mediterranean grub. Apparently our good mate Tony Blair used to be a regular here before he had to move house. Now don't let that sway you, but if it does and you're prepared to spend a night making extremely polite chit-chat amongst Islington's posh folk, you won't be disappointed by the standards.
Tue 6.30-10.30, Wed-Sat 12.30-2.30 then 6.30-10.30, Sun 12.30-3 then 6.30-10
Meal for two: £40 (Chump of lamb)

La Porchetta
141 Upper St, N1 (020) 7288 2488
Angel/Highbury & Islington
Big birthday groups seeking massive, cheap and frankly delicious pizzas need look no further. This place looks really classy and minimal from across the street, but as you get nearer, reveals itself to be anything but – check out the menu design for a start. Real Italian atmosphere and no funny looks as you get increasingly loud and drunken, with house wine at a mere £7.50 a litre. Renditions of 'Happy Birthday' are encouraged, and you'll probably get sparklers in your ice-cream too. Marvellous.
Mon-Sun 12-12
Meal for two: £20 (Pizza Rougala)

Schnecke
80-82 Upper St, N1 (020) 7226 6500
Angel
Essential pre-Schneke advice; make sure you've already had a large three-course meal. The restaurant furniture is straight out of a garden centre, (I'm sure I saw gnomes running around out the back) and unless you have an enigma code-breaking machine to decipher the German border cuisine on the menu,

Roll in...Roll out

you'll have to ask a member of staff. Trouble is they don't have a clue either. So, close your eyes and randomly point at the menu, this will determine your dish. After waiting half an hour with mouth watering, your 'pot luck' meal will arrive. Now, you will have either have received a mound of mashed potato with a rather sizeable German sausage perched on top (lumpy mash, lumpy sausage) or a large, glorified Jacobs cracker with a flavoursome topping of no less than salt and pepper. For a heartier, tastier meal pop down to the local cardboard recycling centre and chomp on an old box. Now, where the hell is KFC?
Mon-Sat 12-12, Sun 12-11.30
Meal for two: £24 (Tarte epinards, a bit like a pizza, with spinach and bacon)

you free mineral water. A classy alternative to your average pizza chains.
Mon-Sat 12-11.30, Sun 12-10.30
Meal for two: £27 (Fiorentina pizza)

Upper St Fish Shop
324 Upper St, N1 (020) 7359 1401
Angel
Recently closed down, previously the finest fish and chips in London. Why oh why?

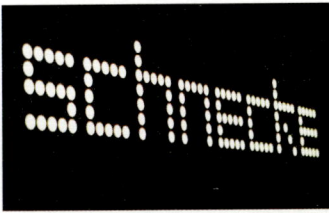

Strada
105-106 Upper St, N1 (020) 7226 9742
Angel
Amazing wood-fired pizzas and a relaxed ambience. The focus here is on quality food, which given that it is a restaurant makes perfect sense. A good place for groups and not too pricey, they even give

wap.itchylondon.co.uk

hoxton & shoreditch

www.itchycity.co.uk

The whole Hoxton/Shoreditch scene started off with arty types moving into the area during the recession, much to the bemusement of the local estates. Bar culture followed suit, and word spread quickly that Hoxton was the next 'new thing'. Nowadays, the place is a mish-mash of style, pretence and out and out fashion victims, providing inspiration for merciless piss-taking but still a number of cracking venues. Take the rough with the smooth and you'll be fine.

Bars

Dragon
5 Leonard St, EC2 (020) 7490 7110
🚇 Old St

Once upon a time, the door policy was

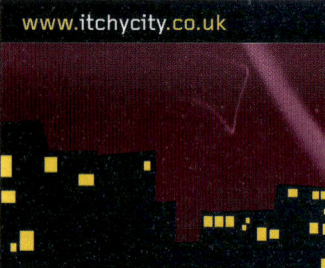

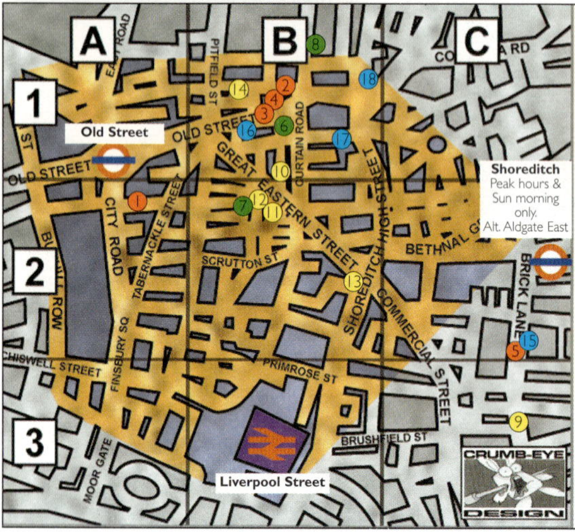

Bars
1. Dragon
2. Hoxton Square Bar & Kitchen
3. Mother/333
4. Shoreditch Electricity Showrooms
5. Vibe Bar

Shoreditch
Peak hours & Sun morning only.
Alt. Aldgate East

Pubs
6. The Bricklayer's Arms
7. Griffin
8. Red Lion

Restaurants
9. Café Naz
10. Cantaloupe
11. The Great Eastern Dining Rooms
12. Home
13. The Light
14. The Real Greek

Clubs
15. 93 Feet East
16. Aquarium
17. Cargo
18. Herbal

born. In Hoxton they decided to reverse it. If you turn up at Dragon in a suit you'll probably be informed that there's a private party going on, and one to which you are not invited. Turn up covered in oil with a hard hat and they'll welcome you into the fold like a long lost mate from art college. Whether you think this sounds like the best idea anyone's ever had, or a load of irritating bollocks, you'll find Dragon a pleasant place to spend the evening. It feels cool, attracts a friendly crowd and you'll never, ever, feel

underdressed. The graffitied toilets can confuse, but once you've worked out if you're Sid or Nancy things get easier. There always seems to be a sofa to sink into, the bar staff are a law unto themselves and it's all pretty entertaining. You've got to check it out really.
Mon-Sat 11-11, Sun 12-10.30

Hoxton Square Bar and Kitchen

2-4 Hoxton Sq, N1 (020) 7613 0709
⊖ Old St

Ever felt like you were invisible? Well, if cool isn't tattooed across your forehead you soon will. You've more chance of getting served by popping next door and bringing it back. Inept bar staff aside, it is a nice bar, especially in the summer when the front opens up onto the square, and you can mingle with the happy people from Bluu who didn't have to wait half an hour for their beer in a plastic pint glass.
Mon-Fri 11-12, Sat 12-12, Sun 12-10.30
Meal for two: £19 (Barbecued chicken sandwich)

Mother

Top floor of 333, 333 Old St, EC1
(020) 7739 5949
⊖ Old St

This place feels like a real discovery. Hidden, with subtle signage, you can't help but feel smug that you're hanging out here while everyone else wanders past oblivious. Hoxtonites like their sofas straight out of a skip, and with these, flocked wallpaper and obscure DJs, they're happy here. Mingle with them, claim to be a designer or an artist, and definitely make some kind of reference to concept graffiti and your hatred for Soho and you'll fit in fine. Don't mention Ikea, your love for Bon Jovi or how much you wish Pitcher and Piano would open a bar in EC1.
Mon-Thu 8-2, Fri-Sat 6-2, Sun 8-2

Find places for late drinks on your WAP
wap.itchylondon.co.uk

hoxton & shoreditch

Elec Showrooms

39a Hoxton Sq, N1
(020) 7739 6934 🚇 **Old St**

No obscure surrealism behind the title; it really did used to be an electricity showroom. Head downstairs to get slaughtered in a room reminiscent of a 70s disco and make some John Travolta moves on the dance floor. Always packed and a genuinely good laugh. Upstairs it's falling over itself to be cool and the novelty bright lights and hospital starkness wear off on the second trip. Still; good for keeping an eye on the 333 queue.
Tue-Wed 12-11, Thu 12-12, Fri-Sat 12-1, Sun 12-10.30
Meal for two: £30 (Duck breast)

Public Life

Commercial St, E1
🚇 **Liverpool St**

This is the hottest newcomer on the Shoreditch block – so hot that no-one knows about it yet. Well, they do now. Formerly an underground public toilet opposite Spitalfields market, there are already numerous 'witty' nicknames flying around, Pubic Lice, for one. In a way though, this is what this bar is all about – pure tongue in cheek – and the talented, artist owner will no doubt be experimenting with art installations. It is rather makeshift, as if they've simply ripped the toilets out and bunged some chairs in – the antithesis of precision planning. Shoreditch bar culture for 2001.

Vibe Bar

The Old Truman Brewery, 91-95 Brick Lane, E1 (020) 7377 2899
🚇 **Aldgate East**

Hot on the heels of the Hoxton scene, Brick Lane is metamorphosing into the place to hang out. And Vibe Bar has got it all; cool venue, innovative DJs, film showings and a chilled out kind of crowd. Perfect for summer weekends when everyone spills out into the courtyard, the red wine flows freely and some deranged looking characters leap around on the dance floor. Thankfully devoid of Hoxton pretension, Vibe is loud, entertaining and deservedly popular.
Mon-Thu 11-11.30, Fri-Sat 11-1.30, Sun 11-10.30

60

www.itchylondon.co.uk

Pubs

The Bricklayer's Arms
63 Charlotte Rd, EC2 (020) 7739 5245
⊖ Old St

In the era of bar culture and the sometimes ridiculous noncery of Shoreditch, it seems like any pub that's this shambolic is 'making a statement'. Take heart though, because although the crowd may be young, fashionable and monied, the place is genuine down to it's roots – it was here way before any of the other bars even clamped eyes on the place. You'll find it filled with the scruffier contingent of Old St cool and the odd androgynous pop star. Upstairs is trying a little harder with an unexpectedly clean and cosy

restaurant corner, alongside extra pub seating. Bricklayers used to be especially renowned for the best Thai food in East Central, however on asking if they still served it I was told with an air of pretension that of course they don't. 'Thai is so out'. Well, nowhere's perfect.

Griffin
93 Leonard St, EC2 (020) 7739 6719
⊖ Old St

Proper pub with proper pub people. Refreshingly normal prices and instead of the faux-shabby chic in the rest of Hoxton's hang-outs – the décor here is genuinely old and falling apart at the seams. Definitely worth a visit. A haven from the scarily cool hoards.

Red Lion
41 Hoxton St, N1 (020) 7739 3736
⊖ Old St

I think the Red Lion is the Red Lion the country over – solid, old-fashioned pub that hasn't changed since the dawn of time. Popular with locals and deservedly so.

Restaurants/Restaurant Bars

Café Naz
46-48 Brick Lane, E1 (020) 7247 0234
⊖ Aldgate East

Contemporary Bangladeshi cuisine, Café Naz stands out a mile amid the rest of Brick Lane's curry houses. Not necessarily a good thing. On the plus side, you get classy décor, Bollywood film clips and an imaginative menu, on the downside, it's expensive and lacks spontaneity. More the kind of place that attracts city types on a night off from Balls Brothers, than hip young things on their way out to EC1. But quality food nonetheless.
Mon-Fri 12-12, Sat-Sun 12-3, 6-12
Meal for two: £22 (Lemongrass chicken)

Cantaloupe
35 Charlotte Rd, EC2 (020) 7613 4411
Old St

Way back when EC1 was da hood, a group of young thangs had the way out idea to convert part of an old factory building in Jack the Ripper territory, into a tapas bar. Four years later, everyone wishes they'd had the idea. As Hoxton folklore goes, Cantaloupe was the first such bar (Bricklayers is a pub don't you know) and it took a long time to get as popular as it is today – so popular that you may have to queue. Don't worry though, there's no nasty door policy and the food really is great.

Mon-Fri 11-12, Sat 2-12, Sun 12-11.30
Meal for two: £35 (Ribeye steak with polenta)

The Great Eastern Dining Rooms
54-56 Great Eastern St, EC2
(020) 7613 4545 Old St

You know Hoxton is past it when people understand what you mean when you say you're going out to the Great Eastern. Most used to think of the spanking new Conran hotel and restaurant/bar multiplex at Liverpool Street., but not any more. Another immensely popular advance booking required-type restaurant. Upstairs is stark and minimal while downstairs is reminiscent of a photo dark room, with light projectors, dingy corners and leather seats. It gets packed and sweaty, but the local crowd love it that way. The kind of place where every second person, you think 'I know them' or 'aren't they that person in...' – don't go and ask for their autograph, you're just pissed and it's dark.

Mon-Fri 12-12, Sat 6.30-12, Restaurant 12.30-3.30 then 6.30-10.45 (Mon-Fri)
Downstairs bar open 'til 1am (Wed-Sat)
Meal for two: £29 (Lemon poached salmon with winter vegetables)

Home
100-106 Leonard St, EC2
(020) 7684 8618
Old St

The restaurant here got so popular that they had to expand. And even with the size increase you'd be wise to book. Super fashionable fusion cuisine in glamorous, relaxed surroundings. After dinner get to grips with the real Hoxton in the basement bar. Here, floppy-haired self-customized jeans meet the asymmetric fringe. Sounds terrifying but really, anything goes, even normal high street stuff (if you're feeling a bit outrageous). The place rocks and the atmosphere is a friendly one.

Mon-Fri 12-12, Sat 6-12, Sun 1-4
Meal for two: £38 (Roast poussin with truffle celeriac mash)

Rolls off the tongue

The Real Greek

15 Hoxton Market, N1 (020) 7739 8212
🚇 **Old St**

Greek food as it should be, and as it so often isn't. Offering lots of small dishes, ideal for ordering en mass and sharing. You won't be disappointed here. The kind of place you could take your visiting holiday romance to remind them of the old country.
Mon-Sat 12-3 then 5.30-12 (Last restaurant orders 10.30)
Meal for two: £30 (Fried squid with olive oil and lemon)

The Light

233 Shoreditch High St
(020) 7247 8989
🚇 **Liverpool St**

The Light is impressive architecturally (a converted power station – thankfully no longer under threat from bulldozers), but other than that, we're not sure what the fuss is all about. A good restaurant, featuring quality seafood and a spacious bar, but a bit devoid of atmosphere. It really is great to look at, and in summer the outdoor seating is somewhat redeeming, but it's just a bit too finely tuned. The kind of place where you feel the need to tidy up after yourself.
Mon-Wed 12-12, Thu-Fri 12-2, Sat 6-2, Sun 12-10.30
Meal for two: £37 (Whole stuffed seabass with clams)

Brick Lane

This colourful East End area, renamed Bangla Town by the Bangladeshi community, offers the ultimate in Indian cuisine. The restaurants are on the whole cheap, often BYO, and for before or after you've got a number of top drawer haunts such as the **Vibe Bar**, all there for the taking. Try **Akash Tandoori** (176 Brick Lane 020 7375 8590), upmarket **Café Naz** (see review) or see who plies most for your trade as you wander through the area.

Clubs

93 Feet East

Truman Brewery, 150 Brick Lane, E1
🚇 **Aldgate East/Liverpool St**

All new live music venue situated in an old Brick Lane music hall. Recently

RIZLA+ It's what you make of it.

You strike me as the active type? Scarlet, 24, Trapeze artist, lives Shep Bush

So where do you circus types get hammered? Bricklayer's Arms

Eating? Too last season? No. I love Fujiyama

How about shopping? Love it. Try the Kite Shop

What makes you stay here? Tate Modern

What'd make you leave? Chris Tarrant

opened and by all means set to be a great success, with a behind the scenes recording studio.

333

333 Old St, EC1 (020) 7739 5949
Old St

Probably the most popular club in these parts and pretty much guarantees a good night. Anywhere that features Pat Sharpe on the wheels of steel (even if it only was for one night) has to be worth a visit. They also publish the Shoreditch Twat fanzine – a half jokey, but actually, still far too serious for its own good, ironic reportage on the latest goings on on Planet Hoxton.

Aquarium

256-260 Old St, EC1 (020) 7251 6136
Old St

A club with a swimming pool – now there's a bit of foresight for you. Aquarium's line-up seems to be ever changing, but one thing's for sure, if you're after legions of gorgeous girls in bikini's you'll be sadly disappointed. If you're after a real party atmosphere, you won't be.

Cargo

83 Rivington St, EC2 (020) 7739 3440
Old St

The newest addition to the land of over-priced and under-laced trainers. Cargo, from the people behind Cantaloupe, recently opened with a bang. It's a bar, restaurant and club with a live music venue and some dodgy sounding sex nights planned. We think it'll fit in well, and with the likes of Beck rumoured to be playing impromtu sets in the coming months, it seems an injection of musical debauchery is set to infiltrate Hoxton.

Herbal

12/14 Kingsland Rd, EC2
Liverpool St

Relative newcomer to the East End club scene set in an old Victorian warehouse. With a small-ish capacity, some great mid-week sessions and the likes of Groove Armada already involved, Herbal looks set to conquer in 2001. Wednesday nights were made for this.

Open seven nights a week 'til 2am.

RIZLA+ www.rizla.com

farringdon & clerkenwell

www.itchycity.co.uk

Bars

19:20

19-20 Great Sutton St, EC1
(020) 7253 1920
⊖ **Farringdon**

Rumour has it that this bar has been Feng Shui'd, which frankly is a relief. Personally I hate it when I turn up somewhere, order a drink and then realise that they've got mirrors in their love corner and the tables are at the wrong angle for karma. Thankfully that won't be a problem here. Red walls, low tables and the obligatory comfy sofas, this is a playground for Clerkenwell's arty types and dot-com dossers.

Mon-Fri 12-11, Sat 6-11

Meal for two: £36 (Caramelised seabass)

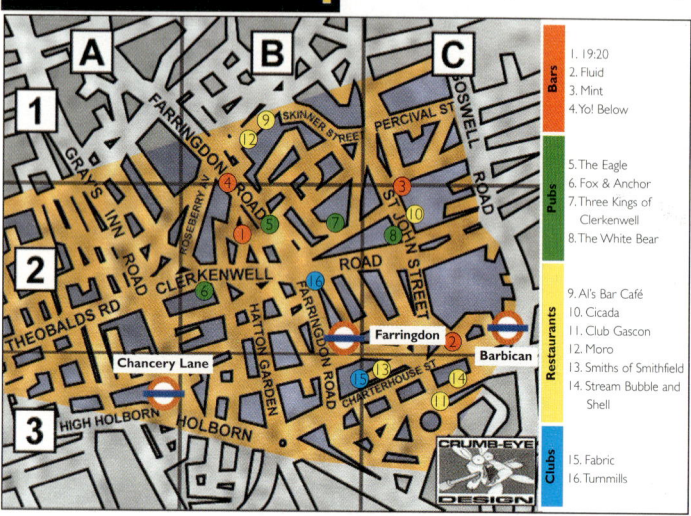

Bars
1. 19:20
2. Fluid
3. Mint
4. Yo! Below

Pubs
5. The Eagle
6. Fox & Anchor
7. Three Kings of Clerkenwell
8. The White Bear

Restaurants
9. Al's Bar Café
10. Cicada
11. Club Gascon
12. Moro
13. Smiths of Smithfield
14. Stream Bubble and Shell

Clubs
15. Fabric
16. Turnmills

Fluid
40 Charterhouse St, EC1 (020) 7253 3444
🚇 Farringdon/Barbican

A bar with a beer vending machine, what could be finer? When the queues are a nightmare, and this place is popular so they inevitably are, you get your loose change out and help yourself. Genius. Fluid is cool; great DJs and kitsch, Japanese influenced interior; fitting, given its sushi menu. And for somewhere that instantly strikes as so hip it hurts, the crowd are refreshingly normal and up for it. Tue-Wed 12-12, Thu-Fri 12-2, Sat 7-2, Sun 12-9. Admission Fri/Sat £3 after 11
Meal for two: £22 (Hand rolled sushi)

Mint

**182-186 St John St, EC1
(020) 7253 8368** 🚇 **Farringdon**

The media has bigged up the Clerkenwell area so much that any empty warehouse in the vicinity is being turned into a bar. Mint opened to quite a press launch, but on our Friday night visit it was near dead for a bar which puts such a so-called happening place to its name. This is a shame as it's a stylish bar, with a good restaurant and much better atmosphere than others in the area. Open late, good DJs, alarmingly cheerful bar staff, and wine tasting 'flights' well worth checking in for.
Mon-Sat 12-12, Sun 12-10.30
Meal for two: £30 (Steak)

Yo! Below
95 Farringdon Rd, EC1 (020) 7841 0785
🚇 Farringdon

Like its Soho counterpart, Yo! offers a novel night out. Sushi, sashimi, karaoke and self-service Kirin. It works well here, offering something different in an area where most of the bars rolled off the same conveyor belt. Hi-tech and super efficient; you can signal the waiters with a mere press of a button – no more stopping your conversation to catch the eye of some bored looking, failed rock star who'd rather be doing coke in the Met Bar. Get horizontal with an attractive specimen on the sofa bed seating at the back, and you might as well spend the night together.
Mon-Sun 12-11

Pubs

The Eagle
159 Farringdon Rd, EC1 (020) 7837 1353
🚇 **Farringdon**

The last word in gastro pub. This is a pub where you could just drink, but it'd be fool-

farringdon & clerkenwell   67

ish not to sample the food. Loud and busy with outdoor seats for the endless, balmy evenings of the great British summer.

Fox & Anchor
115 Clerkenwell St, EC1 (020) 7253 4838
⊖ Barbican/Farringdon

Animal lovers steer well clear. This pub is the preferred stomping ground of Smithfield's meat market fraternity. They start serving early and their breakfasts are fast breakingly fabulous. Brush up on your market banter, if you're after a good deal on a nice bit of sirloin it's a fine place to mingle.
Mon-Fri 7-11

Three Kings of Clerkenwell
7 Clerkenwell Close, EC1 (020) 7253 0483
⊖ Farringdon

Clerkenwell's three kings come bearing a bizarre line in papier maché models, a range of beers and a relaxed, student crowd. All of which we're sure the good lord Jesus would have much preferred.

The White Bear
57 St John St, EC1 (020) 7490 3535
⊖ Farringdon

A good, traditional pub, which on the nights of the week that we've been seems to have been holding some kind of experimental club night. Rumour has it management has changed, and the White Bear massive have moved on elsewhere. Shame, nights like Polar Bear were a perfect pre-Fabric warm up. You can't win 'em all.

Restaurants

Al's Bar Café
11-13 Exmouth Market, EC1
(020) 7837 4821
⊖ Farringdon

Famed for excellent breakfasts, Al's is somewhere you could happily end up at any time of day or night. Hang around after your fry-up, read the papers then treat yourself to one of their burgers for lunch. While you're at it you might as well do dinner and round it all off with a few beers when it turns into a bar later on. Seems Al's got everything covered. What a guy.
Mon-Tue 8-12, Wed-Fri 8-2, Sat 10-2, Sun 10-10.30
All day Breakfast: £6

Cicada
132-136 St John St, EC1 (020) 7608 1550
⊖ Farringdon

A Thai-based restaurant with a fantastic bar, ideal for those nights when you can't quite decide what your priorities are. You'll have a great night here – the

Wind on

unusual menu will tempt even the most jaded of palates, and the bar is never anything but buzzing. A Clerkenwell classic that's well worth checking out.
Mon-Fri 12-11 Sat 6-11
Meal for two: £22 (Clams)

Club Gascon

57 West Smithfield, EC1 (020) 7796 0600
⊖ Barbican
Fantastic French tucker which is casual but posh, modern and cool all at the same time. Famed for its cassoulets and foie gras that blows away anything you've tasted before. Voted the best new restaurant by just about everyone who ever ate here when it opened in '99, it's managed to maintain its bloody high standards. The menu changes with the seasons and they have a fantastic five-course menu for £30 that changes monthly. Well worth it mate, the missus will love it.
Mon-Sat 12-2 7-10 ('til 11 Sat) J.O.
Meal for two: £34 (Grilled Foie Gras with grapes)

Moro

34-36 Exmouth Market, EC1
(020) 7833 8336
⊖ Farringdon/Angel
Spanish North African fusion, which sounds as interesting as it tastes. The menu changes just about everyday so you never know what you're going to get but it's always pukka. Open plan, with the friendliest service in Farringdon and a massively scopey wine list from just about

anywhere with a bit of sun from a tenner bottle of decent French house to a fifty quid Tuscan Chardonnay. Skip the coffee though and nip next door to Café Kick for a beer and a game of table footy. J.O.
Mon-Fri 12.30-2.30 then 7-10.30
Meal for two: £40 (Panfried cod)

Smiths of Smithfield

67-77 Charterhouse St, EC1
(020) 7236 6666
⊖ Farringdon/Barbican
At last the 'next big thing' hangers on and wannabes have moved on, leaving Smiths to the enjoyment of the less fickle amongst us. The breakfasts here are the stuff of legends and the chefs pride themselves on their use of fresh, local produce (can't get fresher than newly slaughtered cows from the nearby meat market). Prices do escalate as you ascend the floors. Behold the Champagne bar where the drinks have an extra price tag which reads 'down with the hoi polloi' – still, this is London.
Mon-Fri 7-10.30, Sat 10.30-10.30, Sun 10.30-10
Meal for two: £30 (Five spiced duck with bok choy (Dining Room menu))

Stream Bubble & Shell

50-52 Long Lane, EC1 (020) 7796 0070
⊖ Barbican

Something a bit different, Stream is a Champagne and shellfish bar and one of a kind in Farringdon. Not somewhere to come if you're a bit common and on a bender, more a classy dinner à deux with someone who knows their lobster eating apparatus. This is not to say that Stream isn't fun. Their own label Champagne is affordable, the menu exciting and the Japanese vending machines downstairs, an irresistible yoyo buying opportunity. Hell, they've even got tropical fish in the toilets – this is definitely one to impress with.
Mon-Fri 12-3 then 3-11, Sat 6-11
Meal for two: £40 (Whole lobster with petit salad)

Clubs

Fabric

77a Charterhouse St, EC1
(020) 7490 0444
⊖ Farringdon

An amazing architectural achievement and no-one can fail to be impressed by the venue itself. (Just try not to think of it as the old 19th century meat cellar it used to be). From the body sonic dance floor (read pumping bass reverberating through your body to give even the most left-footed person a sense of rhythm) to the four-poster beds and unisex toilets, there's enough to keep you entertained even without the music. Which is probably a good job as Fabric's intention to be at the cutting edge of the dance music scene has led to some quite boring DJ sets. But hey, it's a subjective thing, just choose your night carefully, or you may end up in the very unfunny four-hour queue for nothing.

Turnmills

63b Clerkenwell Rd, EC1 (020) 7250 3409
⊖ Farringdon

What? Genuinely friendly door staff, a perfect-sized venue, relaxed dress codes, phenomenal line-ups and short, if any queues? The fickle may have moved on to Fabric, but the early home of the mental Heavenly Social is still one of the most absolutely storming clubs in London. DJs play the place because they love it – a carefully crafted combination of an atmospheric main room, funky-tuned back cellar and perfect chill-out area. After shaky beginnings, Headstart has gained ground as one of Saturday's finest nights. Blinding.

brixton

www.itchycity.co.uk

No-one's afraid of deepest south London anymore as shiny sloanes priced out of SW1 have descended on mass. But, scratch the surface and you'll find the same underground feel that made Brixton what it is. With its unique mix of pub and club with nightlife that never seems to end, Brixton has (unwittingly) inspired many a trend. Accept no imitations...

Bars

Babushka
40 Matthews Road, SW2
(020) 7274 3618
⬤ Brixton

Warm, red and welcoming. Babushka is a chain, but in a good way. There's none of

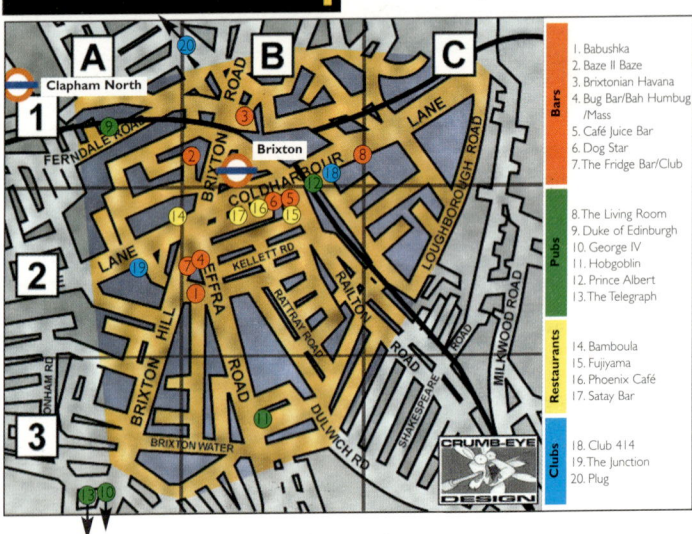

Bars
1. Babushka
2. Baze II Baze
3. Brixtonian Havana
4. Bug Bar/Bah Humbug/Mass
5. Café Juice Bar
6. Dog Star
7. The Fridge Bar/Club

Pubs
8. The Living Room
9. Duke of Edinburgh
10. George IV
11. Hobgoblin
12. Prince Albert
13. The Telegraph

Restaurants
14. Bamboula
15. Fujiyama
16. Phoenix Café
17. Satay Bar

Clubs
18. Club 414
19. The Junction
20. Plug

72 www.itchylondon.co.uk

the ram 'em in, rack 'em up, bleed 'em dry commercialism of your typical All Bar One. A quality, low-key, night out with spot-on music. The ambience is fuelled further by a vast selection of flavoured vodkas and some of the most helpful bar staff in south London.
Mon-Fri 5-11, Fri-Sat 12-12, 12-10.30
Happy hours: Mon-Fri 5-8 (Tue 'bar fly' all day), Sat-Sun 12-8, cocktails £3, vodka shots £1

Baze II Baze
10-12 Tunstall Road, SW9
(020) 7737 4797
Brixton

Mere spitting distance from Brixton tube, Baze is an oasis from the fume-filled high street. It boasts a patio terrace attracting an optimistic, sloaney crowd. Great food by day, and by night a laid-back, loungey vibe with quality salsa, latin and jazz in the basement. And, with over seventy cocktails on offer, there's something to suit the tastes of the most seasoned bar-fly.
Mon-Sun 8.30-12
Meal for two: £25 (Chargrilled chicken with tarragon)

Brixtonian Havana Club
11 Beehive Place, SW9 (020) 7924 9262
Brixton

Far enough from the High Street to appeal to 'those in the know', this place is always rammed. The sort of place where ruffnecks rub shoulders with Tabithas from Cl'am, all in the best possible taste. Décor-wise it's pure Cuban stylee – bright, feel-good and swanky. If you're feeling flush try the infamous 'Brixton riot' cocktail – it'll leave your wallet as light as your head.
Mon-Wed 12-1, Thu-Sat 12-2, Sun 5-12
Meal for two: £38 (Food from a different Caribbean island every month)

Bug Bar
St Matthews Church, Brixton Hill, SW9
(020) 7738 3184
Brixton

Nowhere epitomises the Brixton vibe more than the Bug Bar. Its location in the crypt underneath St Matthews Church is unique in London, and the shabby, youth-club style seating adds flavour to the rabbit-warren, rough 'n' ready feel of the place. The pre-club crowd on a Saturday are your usual suspects – shady characters, scruffy students and E'd up part-timers, while Sunday's jazz-funk and soul nights attract an older crowd. People come here to soak up the place as much as to get down to the music. And where else in London would you find bar staff as chirpy as jobbing actor Vincent, or door-

men as charismatic as legendary bouncer Clifford? Strictly underground.
Mon-Thu 7-1, Fri-Sat 7-3, Sun 7-2
Admission Fri/Sat after 9pm £4, after 11pm £6

Café Juice Bar
407 Coldharbour Lane, SW9
(020) 7738 5528
⊖ **Brixton**

Stepping into this book-lined den feels like you're gate-crashing a film set. The beauty is in the detail – 1970s film posters and retro coffee grinder. The food is similarly authentic – homemade pecan pie and real-fruit smoothies. There's no typical punter really. The Juice Bar is home to a more clued-up breed of Brixtonite seeking solace from the urban pace. Grab a café-latte whilst browsing their vast, second-hand book collection of black history and culture. Look out for their one-off spoken word, live jazz or stand up comedy nights.

Dogstar
389 Coldharbour Lane, SW9
(020) 7737 1016
⊖ **Brixton**

Some say that it was the Dogstar's reputation for messy nights that made Brixton cool. And with cool comes the weekend rent-a-crowd of Carhartt-sporting bright young things. Regardless, the original left-field vibe remains intact, great atmosphere, great music and girls still chat to each other in the toilet queues. Their Sunday roasts are also well worth checking out.
Mon-Thu 12-2.30, Fri-Sat 12-4, Sun 12-2
Admission Fri £3 before 10, £4 before 11, £5 before 12, Sat as Fri but £1 more, Sun £3 after 10.30
Sunday roast: £6.50 (12-6pm)

The Fridge Bar
1 Town Hall Parade, Brixton Hill
London SW2 (020) 7326 5100
⊖ **Brixton**

Despite the decidedly dodgy Changing Rooms décor, this bar is something of a Brixtonian institution. The late licence attracts its fair share of local characters – some look like they've just wandered in from the bus stop. A dimly lit dance floor downstairs encourages just the right amount of sweaty interaction. Just make sure you don't rock up on Goth night.
Mon 9-2.30, Tue-Thu 9-2, Fri-Sat 9-4,

Sun 9-3, Chill-out sessions Sat 5.30am-11am and Sun 5.30am-12pm, Admission Fri/Sat/Sun after 9pm £5/8

The Living Room
433, Coldharbour Lane, SW9
(020) 7326 4040
⊖ **Brixton**

The newest recruit to Brixton's trendy drinking holes at first glance seems like your identikit urban boozer – all low-slung sofas, wooden floors and kitsch, seventies wallpaper. But with a quirky music policy and laid-back clientele, the

Living Room has created a friendly, New-Yorkan mid-week feel. All this changes at the weekend when the place is invaded by totty-seeking shirted lads and an eclectic music policy is jaked in favour of repetitive, four-to-the floor chart nonsense. As is usual with such bars the place starts heaving from about 8pm, which doesn't make for a very authentic living room when you can't even get a bloody chair.
Mon-Sun 5-1

Pubs

Duke of Edinburgh
204 Ferndale Road, SW9
(020) 7924 0509
⊖ **Clapham North/Brixton**

The only place to be on a hot, summer night in Brixton. This pub has a laid-back ambience to rival idyllic, countryside boozers. As such it attracts its fair share of dreadlocked hedgers and crustafarians. You know the types – leftover from the 'Free the Weed' cannabis march in Brockwell Park. But don't fear, the beer garden's big enough to accommodate all varieties of the human gene-pool.
Mon-Thu 12-11, Fri-Sat 12-12, Sun 12-10.30

George IV
144 Brixton Hill, SW2 (020) 8674 5329
⊖ **Brixton**

This pub-club is a proper underground venue. By day it's home to a few sad-looking day-trippers, but at night it comes alive. Home to some legendary techno club nights, including Saturday night, twelve-hour techno marathon, Logic. The casualties seen stumbling out on a Sunday morning are enough to put you off yer roast. For the young at heart we suggest you don your white gloves and be prepared to let it all hang out. This definitely ain't a place for poseurs.
Tue 3-10, Wed-Fri 3-5am, Sat 11-8 then 10-6am, Sun 9pm-5am. Admission charged after 10 at discretion of promoter.

wild weekends www.itchylondon.co.uk

A true Londoner then?
Yep. Ali, 23, Designer, lives Stoke Newington
So tell me where to drink? Dragon
Ah, Hoxton, so you'll be showing off your ironic t-shirts later? Not exactly. But for clubbing I like Fabric
And where d'you buy 'em?
Shut up about t-shirts. Spitalfields is good
Why do you love the capital? It's never boring
Any complaints? Door policies annoy me

Hobgoblin
95 Effra Rd, SW2 (020) 7501 9671
🚇 **Brixton**

A bit of a trek from Brixton centralis, but well worth the walk, especially in the summer for the vast beer garden. What with the bona-fide rustic wooden seating, free entry, 2am licence and booming sound system, you could almost imagine you're at Glastonbury... almost. The back bar or conservatory hosts a variety of arty events from stand-up comedy and spoken-word to salsa. Full-on festival feeling and best of all, no-ones peddling you patchouli oil.
Mon-Thu 2-12, Fri-Sat 12-2, Sun 2-12

Prince Albert
418 Coldharbour Lane, SW9
(020) 7274 3771
🚇 **Brixton**

No fancy cocktails, big-name DJs or local celebrities. Hell, they've only stocked vodka/Red Bull since the summer. Landlady Pat is not a woman for fads, so there's no chance of a trance nation night springing up here. The Albert is your good, old-fashioned boozer – with décor reminiscent of an out-of-town Harvester and KP dry roasted peanuts for bar snacks. It attracts an unfashionably friendly crowd who are as loyal as they are appreciative of the eclectic (read dodgy) music policy. It doesn't even have a late licence, encouraging intelligent conversation and 'back to mine' after-parties. Far more agreeable than caning it into the early hours, dontcha think?

The Telegraph
228 Brixton Hill, SW2 (020) 8671 5164
🚇 **Brixton**

The Telegraph is the Brixtonian pub-cum-club du jour. All the elements are there – the dodgy 1970's décor, the ever-so-slightly-off the beaten track location miles up Brixton Hill and the fact that it's the location for Basement Jaxx's newest night 'Rooty'. Really, it's just your bog-standard boozer, with a handy, sweaty backroom. File under 'next big thing'. And hurry before the wannabe hair-flicking hordes move in.
Mon-Thu 11-11, Fri-Sat 11-4am, Sun 12-

Cheap meal offers sent to your phone
wap.itchylondon.co.uk

10.30 Admission at discretion of promoter Fri/Sat after 10pm, approx £5

Restaurants

Bah Humbug
The Crypt, St Matthews Church, SW9 (020) 7738 3184
Brixton
The prices are far from cheap but Bah Humbug's definitely worth it. The fairy lights and religious artefacts lend the place a distinctly ethereal ambience. Perhaps a bit over the top with Mary Magdalene on the front cover of the menu, but hey, at least the place has got character. Perfect for romantic tête-a-têtes. They do a great selection of savoury crêpes and a cholesterol-defying veggie brunch on a Sunday, with ingredients fresh from Brixton market. Lovely.
Mon-Sat 5-12, Sun 11-12

Meal for two: £30 (Crispy Cantonese mock duck)

Bamboula
12 Acre Lane, SW2 (020) 7737 4144
Brixton
A trip down Brixton way wouldn't be complete without sampling a few Caribbean cafés. And by all accounts this does the best Caribbean cuisine in Brixton. We recommend their jerk chicken, although the whole damn menu is pretty fantastic. Colourful, cheerful and won't break the bank. What are you waiting for?
Mon-Fri 11-11, Sat 12-11, Sun (open every other week) 12-4

Meal for two: £20 (Jerk chicken)

Fujiyama
7 Vining Street, SW9 (020) 7737 2369
Brixton

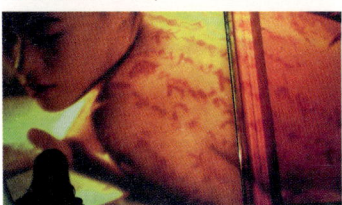

Fine Japanese cuisine. This long-running restaurant cleans up in the style-meets-top-nosh stakes. They also play host to some outlandish nights – when I popped in last there was either some kind of Celtic karaoke or druid cult induction going on in the room upstairs. Things are infinitely more sedate downstairs – the perfect environment in which to kick back with a glass of sake.
Mon-Thu 12-11, Fri-Sat 12-12, Sun 12-11

Meal for two: £18 (Yaki Udon, prawn noodles)

Phoenix Café
441 Coldharbour Lane, SW9 (020) 7733 4430
Brixton
The Phoenix Café is a welcome haven from the stark minimalism of newer eateries. This is your no-frills, greasy spoon specialising in what Jamie Oliver would call 'pukka' sarnies and all-day fried breakfasts. Proper food at decent prices. Try to avoid the lunch hour rush – it's quick service but it ain't McDonalds.
Mon-Sat 6.30am-5. Unlicensed.

All day breakfast: £3.50

The Satay Bar
447-455 Coldharbour Lane, SW9
(020) 7326 5001
⬤ **Brixton**

Atmospheric bar/restaurant frequented by a friendly, mixed crowd of local players, wide boys and glammed-up preppies. The décor is inviting, bar the scary looking Indonesian voodoo dolls nailed to the walls. Food-wise the menu is a mix of Malaysian, Indonesian and Singaporean offerings. Come here to trade gags with Harry, the charismatic owner/manager whilst supping an appropriately named 'Zombie Killer' cocktail. Just mind the step on the way out.
Mon-Fri 12-11, Sat 1-12, Sun 1-10.30
Meal for two: £20 (Ayam spicy fish)

Clubs

Club 414
414 Coldharbour Lane, SW9
⬤ **Brixton**

Small, dark club hosting DJs such as Colin Dale, Mr C and Terry Francis. Recently nominated 'the worst club in Britain' (probably by some shit style mag) – 414 is a welcome antidote to bland, overpriced, magnolia-walled super-clubs. It offers a decidedly un-cool music policy – check out such mind boggling musical genres as 'Uplifting Hardgaba House' and 'Psychedelic Techno Trance'. At least you can rest assured a night out here won't be spent dodging Psion-organised fashion victims.

The Fridge Club
1 Town Hall Parade, Brixton Hill
(020) 7326 5100
⬤ **Brixton**

Still basking in the glory of it's infamous late nineties techno-trance fests, the Fridge deals out the same speed 'n' seed formula as it did five years ago. And why not? If it ain't broke then don't fix it. True, they're still popular, but the cracks are beginning to show. Prices have gone up, water taps are turned off to a trickle and

Less taxing roll

punters are being packed in 'til there's no room to punch the air. And, then there's the bonus of security so moody they'd make Mr T quake in his Adidas. With the ever-increasing local competition, beware the fall out.

The Junction
242, Coldharbour Lane SW9
(020) 7647 7615, (020) 7274 6696
🚇 **Brixton**

The Junction is something of a victim of it's own Basement Jaxx-fuelled success. Barely had the paint dried on the newly refurbished ceiling than the Brixton party massive had moved onto venues new. Sadly, unless you're a day-glo clubber of the Gatecrasher variety it just ain't happening. I had the misfortune of turning up there one Saturday at 7am to scenes of euphoria last witnessed in Inspector Morse goes to a rave. Except these were more clichéd – tops off, glo-sticks and free bananas. Avoid.

TOP FIVE
Serious Clubbing
1. Fabric (p71)
2. The End (p31)
3. Home (p41)
4. Turnmills (p71)
5. The Fridge Club (p78)

Mass
St Matthews Church, Brixton Hill SW9
(020) 7771 7099
🚇 **Brixton**

Once the buzzing king of the Brixton club scene, Mass wins hands down in terms of venue. Sadly the crowd ain't what it used to be. Dreary students dancing enthusiastically to drum 'n' bass. Mass is too big to be intimate – everyone's off on their own tip. Still, if you're more into the DJ line up than the party, you'll be happy as a pig in a limitless field of shit.

The Plug
90 Stockwell Road, SW9
(020) 7771 7099
🚇 **Stockwell**

Situated in the less-than-salubrious environs of Stockwell – The Plug attracts a spill-over Brixton crowd seeking less obvious entertainment. What makes this place are the specialist nights, changing crowd and welcoming staff. If you find yourself in Stockwell one evening, you could do a lot worse.

RIZLA It's what you make of it.

brixton

clapham

www.itchycity.co.uk

Clapham's identity is slowly being squeezed out by the invasion of the ubiquitous, pine-furnished bar chain. But amid the Fulham overflow and mass house-buying mania, enough of its old charm remains. Conceivably, we could write a whole book on Clapham, there's that much choice. Here's a sample of some of the finer choices...

Bars

Arch 635

15-16 Lendal Terrace SW4 (020) 7720 7343
🚇 **Clapham North**

After changing hands just over a year ago, Arch 635 has become one of Clapham's best-kept secrets. Part-owner Shane Ranasinghe puts its new-found

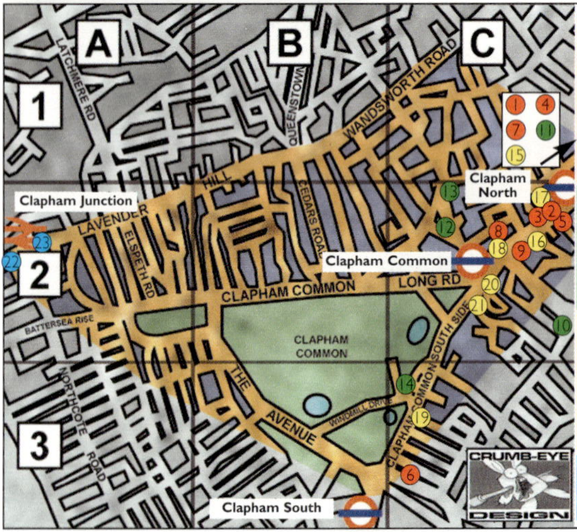

Bars
1. Bar Arch 635
2. Bierodrome
3. Café Sol
4. Circle Bar
5. Loaffers
6. Oblivion
7. Sand
8. The Sequel
9. So:uk

Pubs
10. 100
11. The Falcon
12. Frog & Forget-me-not
13. The Sun
14. Windmill on the Common

Restaurants
15. Alba
16. Eco
17. El Rincon Latino
18. Gastro
19. Hornimans
20. Pepper Tree
21. Tiger Lil's

Clubs
22. The Clapham Grand
23. Wessex House

popularity down to the friendly atmosphere they promote, and it certainly seems to have paid off; receiving bar industry recognition. The (gradually) refurbished venue is packing them in. And, with a music policy centred around funk and soul and a hangover-inducing happy hour, Arch 635 seems to have achieved that obvious but rare combination of booze, good music and a crowd who are basically up for having a laugh.
Mon-Fri 5-11, Sat 12-12, Sun 12-10.30

Bierodrome

44-48 Clapham High St. SW4
(020) 7720 1118
Clapham Common/Clapham North
As the title suggests, the main attraction of the Bierodrome is the gargantuan selection of obscure beers and lagers on offer. Be careful what you choose, as some of these drinks have the potency of bleach. And, if you do steer clear of them, you might just last long enough to appreciate the ski chalet come log cabin bar design. An unlikely scenario, but still.

Mon-Wed 12-12, Thu 12-1, Fri-Sat 12-2, Sun 10.30-2
Meal for two: £25 (Belgo mussel pot with frites)

Café Sol

56 Clapham High Street, SW4
(020) 7498 9319
Clapham North
The cheesiest venue in town and the most fun, making it numero uno for late night boozing and a guaranteed snog. This tacky Mexican restaurant/bar throbs into the early hours every weekend as a surreal mix of people squeeze into every available nook and cranny to dance, drink and feel each other up. Classy it ain't, but what the hell, they serve a mean margarita and you can dance on the tables.
Mon-Thu, Sun 12.30-1, Fri-Sat 12.30-2,
Meal for two: £25 (Nachos)

Circle Bar

348 Clapham Road, SW9
(020) 7622 3683
Clapham North/Stockwell
The only redeeming feature of this bar is that it sells Absinthe. The potent green

THE INDEPENDENT ON SUNDAY — The best writers, the sharpest opinions

spirit is guaranteed to make you forget about the rude bar staff and dodgy location. Weekend DJs give it a certain credibility and being virtually the only bar in the vicinity it manages to do pretty well.
Mon-Sat 11-11, Sun 11-10.30

Loaffers

102-104 Clapham High Street, SW4
(020) 7720 9596
 Clapham Common/Clapham North

Offering an interesting contrast of décor, the Loaffers bar features stylish beech and red leather alongside a restaurant, which is pure Barratt show-home. If you're looking for some dado-rail tips this could well be the place for you. Otherwise, best stick to the bar. One of those places that aims to cater for every social need of your average discerning Claphamite, the principal being to Loaf and eat, Loaf and drink, Loaf and generally look attractive. Sadly it's all a bit 'been done before'.
Mon-Fri 12-11, Sat 11-11, Sun 12-10.30
Meal for two: £25 (Crab and Coriander Coconut Cakes with Sweet Chilli Salsa)

Oblivion

7-8 Cavendish Parade, Clapham Common Southside, SW4
(020) 8772 0303
 Clapham South

Populated by attractive late-twenty-pushing-thirty-somethings, this is your typical, trendy Clapham bar. Fairly average, except the (excuse momentary immaturity) random bronze bottoms and breasts decorating the bar and semi-naked men and women plastered all over the loos. Good crack on a Sunday afternoon when it's packed with punters squeezing the last drops of enjoyment out of the weekend.
Mon-Sun 12-11
Meal for two: £28 (Steak)

Sand

156 Clapham Park Road, SW4
(020) 7622 3022
 Clapham Common/Brixton

Sand is an oasis in the desert that surrounds the High Street. Lounge on sofas and sip delectable cocktails by flickering candle light – and if that gets a little tiresome, watch a classic movie on one of the many mini TVs embedded in the walls. Never before has Clapham seen such fabulous interior design and skillful

mixology. Unfortunately, its resulting popularity makes for long queues at the weekends. Patience and suitable attire (as per bouncers whim) are required to make it inside. Once you've endured this, things are looking up – DJs play wickedly funky tunes and pulling potential is sky high. Weeknights offer a toned down ambience – equally indulgent but a bit more sedate.
Mon-Sat 5-2, Sun 5-1
Meal for two: £39 (Roast seabass)

The Sequel
75 Venn Street, SW4 (020) 7622 4222
⊖ **Clapham Common**

A slick, stylish bar and restaurant tucked away off the High Street. Attractive (always a bonus), attentive staff and groovy music combine to transport you into a world of class, style and sophistication. But only momentarily, as your eyes are drawn to the enormous television screen that sits above the bar. On our visit, Bugs Life was playing – we can only hope as a result of some kind of bizarre freak accident.
Mon-Fri 5-11, Sat 11-11, Sun 11-10.30
Meal for two: £34 (Caramelised onion tart)

So:uk
165 Clapham High Street, SW4
(020) 7622 4004
⊖ **Clapham Common**

The laddish camaraderie of Men Behaving Badly and the sleek, mod styling of Quadrophenia? Unfortunately, Leslie Ash's So:uk bar on Clapham High Street includes none of the elements of her colourful acting career. However, its combination of inviting soft things to sit on and a DJ situated in the middle of the bar area makes the whole experience a bit like going round your mates house, albeit one with far too many friends and a degree in interior design. Its tempting menu ensures daytime popularity to boot.
Mon-Sun 11-12
Meal for two: £34 (Wok-fried beef with warm noodle salad)

Pubs

100
100 Clapham Park Road, SW4
(020) 7720 8902
⊖ **Clapham Common**
The 100 pub has that much sought-after

local vibe that so many Clapham haunts are trying to achieve. You'll find it off the beaten track and squaring up to one of Clapham's better estates. When they are not serving food from the pizza menu you can pop next door for a Chinese and eat it in the bar, and the staff have also been known to supply lost-property orphan umbrellas at closing time. Ahh.

The Falcon
33 Bedford Rd, SW4 (020) 7274 2428
Clapham Common/Clapham North
An old favourite, warm and welcoming in winter, with an enormous beer garden to abuse in summer. Having recovered from the trauma of finding their pool table removed about six months ago, we are now ready to sing The Falcon's praises once more. It serves reasonable Thai food and best of all, does cashback at the bar, so you can have that extra pint without having to haul ass to Clapham Common.

Frog and Forget-me-not
The Pavement, SW4 (020) 7622 5230
Clapham Common
Want to go to the pub, but can't bear to leave your living room? Well, at the Frog and Forget-me-not, you can experience the home comforts of an open fire, comfy sofa and a token feline known affectionately to the locals as 'Marmalade'. The Frog provides the perfect lazy Sunday antidote for a weekend of indulgence with its warm, welcoming surroundings. Most people just turn up and fall into a sofa and the Frog is the kind of place where they would rather give you a quilt for the night than throw you out come closing time.

Sun
47 Clapham Old Town SW4 (020) 7622 4980
Clapham Common Tube
A Mediterranean-style pub and a huge summer attraction with its heated courtyard. It's all a bit try-hard trendy – you'll find yourself fighting for wonky wooden seats with city boys and people who pronounce Clapham 'Clarm' (does that make Streatham St Reatham?). All the strutting and posturing makes for a rather uncomfortable evening in my opinion, then again, I am paranoid and un-cool.

cheap eats — www.itchylondon.co.uk

Windmill on the Common

Windmill Drive, SW4 (020) 8673 4578
Clapham Common

The Windmill is bloody enormous and one of the few, truly traditional British pubs (but for the obligatory Aussie staff), left in Clapham. Perfect for boozing on a sunny summer's afternoon. Everyone spills out on to the common to laze in the sunshine, soak up the unique South London atmosphere and check out the talent. And hell, there's a lot of talent.

Restaurants

Alba Pizzeria

3 Bedford Road, SW4 (020) 7733 3636
Clapham North

The best goddamn pizza I've ever had, and boy I've had a few. The fantastic food and tiny dining room mean you have to take your chances and squeeze onto a table when and where you can. This only adds to the atmosphere, which without meaning to gush, is bloody fantastic and presided over with style by the charismatic owner. It is your duty to try the traditional calzone, or die having never tasted true perfection.

Eco

162 Clapham High Street
(020) 7978 1108
Clapham Common

Plastic-wrapped and feeling like new shoes that need walking in, Eco is a popular meeting point, being close to Clapham Common tube and The Picture House. Not the kind of place that you can melt into for the night though – bookings are run with scary precision. All in all a clichéd, trendy pizzeria. Good for large groups and birthdays.
Mon-Fri 12-4 then 6.30-11, Sat 12-5 then 6-11.30, Sun 12-5 then 6-11
Meal for two: £25 (La Dolce Vita, pizza)

El Rincon Latino

148 Clapham Manor Street, SW4
(020) 7622 0599
Clapham North

Proper Spanish style tapas restaurant. Great atmosphere and the kind of ridiculously accommodating staff who'll forgive you when you and your mates get trashed on Sangria and break things.
Mon-Fri 10-12, Sat 11-12, Sun 11-11
Meal for two: £25 (tapas)

Gastro

67 Venn St, SW4 (020) 7627 0222
Clapham Common

A slice of France cunningly planted in the middle of Clapham, serving delicious food from dawn 'til dusk. The owner hails from Brittany and specialises in traditional, regional dishes including rabbit stew, black pudding and an awe-inspiring seafood platter. Sit at the communal table and chat to the endlessly entertaining

mix of clientele, or just relax and watch the world go by through a smoky haze. Many a wild night has started here – you never know, you might end up at Madame Jo Jo's with the chef.
Mon-Sun 8-12
Meal for two: £30 (Poached salmon)

Hornimans

69 Clapham Common Southside, SW4
(020) 8673 9162
Clapham Common

The dramatic entrance, complete with Olympic flames and canvas awning raises the expectations just that little bit too high. However, it's a cosy kind of place with a reasonably priced menu. Its saving grace has to be the weeknight happy hour from 4-7pm, which attracts a nice mix of cheapskates. Relax beneath the grand canopy on a summer's eve, take in the view of Clapham Common, keep the cut price beers coming and you'll soon forget the traffic roaring past.
Mon-Fri 4-12, Sat 10-12, Sun 10-11
Meal for two: £34 (Honey glazed duck)

The Pepper Tree

19 Clapham Common Southside, SW4
(020) 7622 1758
Clapham Common

The kind of interior you would usually associate with fast food chain restaurants, and with similar queues. The canteen-style tables are great for sociable types, but not the ideal place to treat your mates to a blow-by-blow account of your latest conquest. Add tasty Thai cuisine and you're onto a winner – the ideal kebab stand alternative for the discerning inebriated diner that lies within all of us.
Mon 12-3 then 6-10.30, Tue-Sat 12-3 then 6-11, Sun 12-10.30
Meal for two: £20 (Thai green curry)

Tiger Lil's

16a Clapham Common Southside, SW4
(020) 7720 5433
Clapham Common

Tiger Lil's is a Mongolian style, pick-your-own-food-and-let-the-chef-cook-it-no-matter-how-random-the-combination type restaurant with open plan kitchens. A lively atmosphere, instilled by animated

Roll on

www.itchylondon.co.uk

Explain yourself. Louise, 22 Australian traveller lives Mile End

An Aussie. So you work in a pub then? No, but I drink in the Elbow Room.

Where's good for a barbie? Look, I survive without them, I eat at Strada.

And after a day's hard yakka, clubbing? I love Home. It's better in Sydney though.

I guess you hate London's weather? Not bothered. I love tea. Hate the tube.

chefs who delight in preparing your selected delicacies over the kind of flames usually associated with a 5-10 stretch for arson. Still, you go to a restaurant so someone else can cook for you – not to choose something crap yourself. Far too much scope for error.
Mon-Thu 6-11.30, Fri 6-12, Sat 12-12, Sun 12-11

Meal for two: £33 (Unlimited stir-fry)

Clubs

Clapham Grand
Grand Theatre, 21-25 St John's Hill SW11 (020) 7228 1070
≷ Clapham Junction

Not strictly Clapham, but one of the places you're likely to end up at after a night in the area. Its setting in an old theatre brings new meaning to the phrase 'and they were dancing in the aisles'. You will be, you'll be absolutely wasted, revelling in chart pop and finding virtually everyone attractive. A night at the Grand is the stuff of legends. The kind where you wake up the next morning in some bizarre Greater London suburb, wearing someone else's clothes. And be warned the queues are massive.

Wessex House
1a St John's Hill, SW11 (020) 7228 0501
≷ Clapham Junction

For those who can't face the queues and prices at the Grand (and a few die-hard fans who, well, just like it). Classy it isn't, nor dressy, nor sophisticated, nor glamorous. But that's kind of the whole point. A shonky, steamingly-hot bar adjoins an ice-cold dance floor in this post-pub can't-be-bothered with pleasantries, down-to-earth celebration of all things anti-Clapham. A hole to some, heaven to others.

RIZLA+ www.rizla.com

clapham

fulham

www.itchycity.co.uk

Trust fund central. If you're young and pretty with a gold card at your disposal you more than likely hang out here. Likewise a mixture of well to do families and young professionals who have never been east of Soho. Fulham is a classy part of town, posh shops, fast cars and the kind of debauched behaviour that comes with knowing that your cash flow will never dry up. Take it for what it is and enjoy. One word of warning though – unlike the other areas in this book, Fulham doesn't handily fall into one section – walking from one cluster of bars to the other can take you a good half hour. Take the 211 bus to get up the Fulham Road or the number 11 for the Kings Road. Catch both outside the tube station.

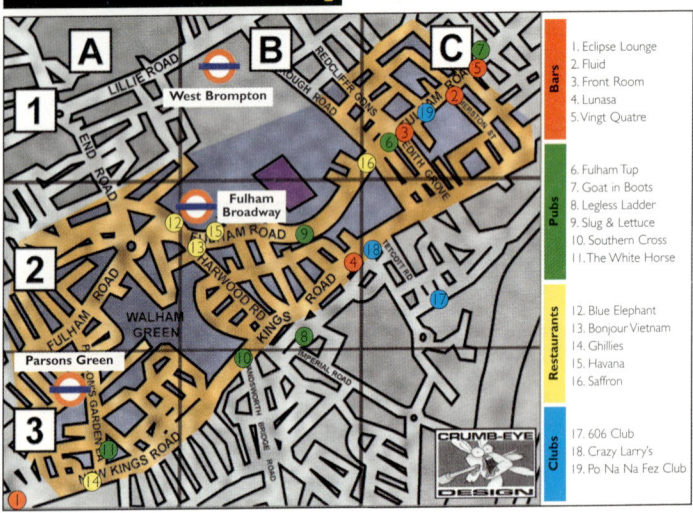

Bars
1. Eclipse Lounge
2. Fluid
3. Front Room
4. Lunasa
5. Vingt Quatre

Pubs
6. Fulham Tup
7. Goat in Boots
8. Legless Ladder
9. Slug & Lettuce
10. Southern Cross
11. The White Horse

Restaurants
12. Blue Elephant
13. Bonjour Vietnam
14. Ghillies
15. Havana
16. Saffron

Clubs
17. 606 Club
18. Crazy Larry's
19. Po Na Na Fez Club

88 www.itchylondon.co.uk

Bars

Eclipse Lounge
108-110 New Kings Road, SW6
(020) 7731 2142
🚇 **Parsons Green/Putney Bridge**
Recently refurbed, reliably well-mixed cocktails served in a relaxed, dimly-lit, smoky bar. Food is good and well priced (a main course comes in at around £8). Chilled music completes the feel. Often empty on weekdays, it's Friday and Saturday nights when it comes into its own.
Mon-Sat 12-11, Sun 12-10.30
Meal for two: £22 (Pork and herb sausages with mash)

Fluid
208 Fulham Road, SW10 (020) 7352 4372
🚇 **Fulham Broadway**

A juice bar with décor so chic and inviting that you may find yourself drawn to it. Beware, o pisshead, for verily this is a healthy place. The smoothies and freshly squeezed juices, all organic, are gorgeous beyond compare. Recommended for those cold winter months is the hot organic apple juice with cinnamon and spices. Liquid heaven. A few shots of vodka wouldn't go amiss, mind.

Front Room
246 Fulham Rd, SW10
(020) 7823 3011 🚇 **Fulham Broadway**
Packed with your obligatory Fulham rugby boys, but chilled and sophisticated enough to deter them from taking their trousers off. A friendly feel and a hangover defying breakfast menu make this a popular place for the morning after as well as the night before. A fine choice.
Mon-Sat 12-11, Sun 12-10.30
Breakfast: £6

Lunasa
575 Kings Rd, SW7
(020) 7371 7664 🚇 **Fulham Broadway**
One of the best bars in the area. Classy types downing vodkas at unprecedented rates and mingling over a bottle of Stella. The atmosphere at Lunasa is always buzzing, the bar staff phenomenally attractive and the décor stylish. In fact, we can't think of a single bad thing to say about the place. Not one. Honestly, you'd think it was owned by the reviewer's best mate from primary school or something.
Mon-Sun 4-11.30
Meal for two: £10 (Salad nicoise)

fulham

89

Vingt Quatre

325 Fulham Road, SW10
(020) 7376 7224
🚇 **Fulham Broadway**

Essentially, a shotgun shack with a run-of-the-mill minimalist makeover that is starting to look very dated, very quickly. That aside, the place is clean and the food of a high standard. It is permissible to just drink but, taking into account the prohibitive prices (£3.30 for a Becks) and the less than inspiring atmosphere, there are plenty of other places around to slake a thirst in style. For 24 hour food, though, definitely worth a look.

Open 24hrs
Meal for two: £27 (Fish cakes)

Pubs

Fulham Tup

268 Fulham Road, SW10
(020) 7352 1859 🚇 **Fulham Broadway**

One of a chain, not renowned for its subtlety, this is a lively pub catering for the youngsters of the area. With a huge screen, sports-fans are well served, but the rest of you might want to try somewhere a little more interesting. Pub grub is good but, like the establishment itself, nothing to go overboard about.

Goat in Boots

333 Fulham Road, SW10
(020) 7352 1384 🚇 **Fulham Broadway**

Room

An impressive layout of inter-connecting snugs give this pub a cosy feel. Ideal for large-ish groups looking to relax in each other's company, rather than hunting parties on the pull. Clientele is young and monied, anybody over thirty seems to be a groovy boss showing the office juniors what a gold card looks like. Thursday's the night if you like your vodka shots, as they drop from their not unreasonable £2 to a quid. With other drinks coming in at a similar price band, including well-shaken cocktails, this is a good place to spend an evening. And for anyone wanting to go on past last orders, recently opened upstairs is the members-only nightclub, imaginatively called 'Room'.

www.itchylondon.co.uk

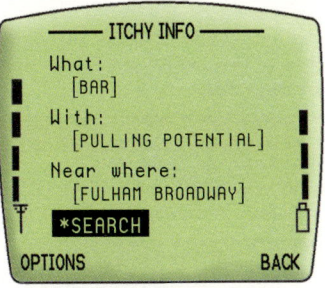

**Hot dates
direct to your WAP
wap.itchylondon.co.uk**

Legless Ladder
1 Harwood Terrace, SW6 (020) 7610 6131
⊖ Fulham Broadway
Old fashioned, log fire kind of place, quiet during the week, and packed with loud, drunken Fulhamites at weekends. As a result it's a pretty much perfect choice whatever your mood, just so long as you pick your timing.

Slug and Lettuce
474 Fulham Rd, SW6 (020) 7385 3209
⊖ Fulham Broadway
Does exactly what it says on the tin. Not that I mean you get a free curled-up leaf upon which resides a snail-like mollusc with a rudimentary internal shell and a severe aversion to salt, but that it's a chain pub, innit? Yes, they have a flunky washing your hands in the toilet, but it can't shake off its spit 'n' sawdust Club 18-30 holiday feel. At any time of the day or night, it feels as though it's been filled with ten coach loads of lager-fuelled twats who think they're in Blackpool. Pure class.

Southern Cross
65 New Kings Road, SW6 (020) 7736 2837
⊖ Fulham Broadway
Unfussy decor that's all chalk-boards and special offers, does no justice to what is actually a damn fine pub. Your beer has a head, the staff are courteous, the jukebox well-stocked and (always nice to know), the Sloanes, Trustafarians and Yardies don't go near it. An A-board outside boasts 'the finest food in Fulham.' That's pushing it a bit, but in its price range, I don't think the trading standards people need to call round just yet.

The White Horse
**No. 3 Parsons Green, SW6
(020) 7736 2115**
⊖ Parsons Green
One of the best pubs in London, the White Horse's reputation draws people from all over. Known locally as 'the Sloaney Pony', it will come as no surprise that solicitors, estate agents and Notting Hillbillies make up a fair share of the clientele. It isn't exclusive or snooty, or anything close, but a genuinely friendly place. Staff are relaxed, happy and well-trained, getting a bad pint is as rare as seeing Halley's comet. Prices are surprisingly low, with a special mention deserved for the spirits. There are a hell of a lot of them on offer and they all, with a few exceptions, cost £2 a shot. Bad news if you're a fan of cheap vodka, but

great if you and your mates fancy a Glenfiddich marathon. Packed all year round, it's especially worth a visit during the summer months when the woody scent from the outdoor barbecue is on the breeze. Six slow pints, a hefty burger and the sun going down over the Green... you'll sleep well that night, believe me.

Restaurants/Restaurant Bars

Blue Elephant

4-6 Fulham Broadway, SW6
(020) 7385 6595
Fulham Broadway

Sumptuous food served in surroundings to match, this is one of the best Thai restaurants around. Constantly recommended in top ten London restaurants type guide books, we had to give it a mention. And one that is well deserved. Prices verge on over the top, and being so close to the tube, tables are often hard to come by. Booking in advance would be prudent.
Mon-Sun 12-2.30 then 7-12
Meal for two: £40 (Chuchi koong – a dry curry dish)

Bonjour Vietnam

593-599 Fulham Road, SW6
(020) 7385 7603
Fulham Broadway

Superb South-East Asian food and an excellent level of service. With a sliding scale on the menu, the earlier in the week you eat, the less it costs. Even so, at weekends, the bill won't exactly shock and is well worth it considering the standard of the cuisine.
Mon-Thu 12-2.30 then 6-11, Fri-Sat 12-2.30 then 6-11.30, Sun 12-3 then 6-10.30
Meal for two: £30-£40 (All you can eat set menu, price rises at weekends)

Ghillies

271 New Kings Road, SW6 (020) 7371 0434
Fulham Broadway

The informal and bar-like appearance of

Hot tip

this small restaurant belies the fact that it is one of the best seafood joints in the area. Serves a range of other dishes aside from fish, all at a very high standard, and is used by the locals as a bar. Fish and chips are available to take away and come recommended, although at £8, they'd have to be. A little gem of a plaice.
Mon-Fri 9-10.30, Sat 9.30-10.30, Sun 9.30-3

Meal for two: £60 (Fruits de mer with lobster – admittedly we have chosen the most expensive thing on the menu here – there are plenty of cheaper options)

Havana
490 Fulham Rd, SW6 (020) 7381 5005
⊖ Fulham Broadway
The grotesque exterior doesn't, unfortunately, mask hidden treasures within. This is a ghastly, alcopops-quaffing, tack-fest, with all the class and charm of the nightclub you used to go to when you were fourteen. It does serve decent tapas, though if you want to enjoy them take

TOP FIVE...
Funk/Soul/Jazz
1. **Notting Hill Arts Club (p101)**
2. **606 Club (p95)**
3. **Living Room (p75)**
4. **Ronnie Scott's (p16)**
5. **Bar Rumba (p40)**

along some ear-plugs. Pumping chart handbag and 'sexy Latin beats' ain't known for aiding digestion.
Mon-Sat 12-2, Sun 12-10.30 Admission £5 after 9 £8 after 10 Wed £3
Tapas: from £4.50

Saffron
306b Fulham Road, SW10
(020) 7565 8183
⊖ Fulham Broadway
Indian cuisine as the ex-pats of pre-Independence Bombay may have experienced it. The small, almost cramped, reception area on the ground floor feels more English living-room than curry house. The art adorning the walls are inoffensive Pollock-esque canvases, rather than the usual startled tiger. Stairs lead up to an exclusive dining area, with drapes and colourful curtains, giving the impression that you're dining aboard a cruise ship. The food itself is utterly fantastic. Whether these are the best surroundings in which to scoff curry depends largely on whether you were born closer to Bradford than

RIZLA + It's what you make of it.

And you are?
William, 31, Art student, lives Forest Hill
Where do you paint the town red?
The Crown & Anchor
And then go for some artistic perspiration? Electric Ballroom usually
I like your style... where d'you get it?
Yesterday's Bread
London, love it? Yes – it's not up north
Worst thing? Cabs don't run south of river

Basingstoke. A tip for visiting northerners: they don't serve lager in cans at four in the morning.
Mon-Sun 12-3 then 6-12
Meal for two: £21 (Chicken tikka masala)

Clubs

606 Club
90 Lots Rd, SW10 (020) 7352 5953
Ⓤ Fulham Broadway
Members jazz club for genuine aficionados only – the music's serious, the atmosphere's smoky and the punters know their stuff. Definitely not a place to show off knowledge gained from 'The Best Jazz Album in the World...Ever' but somewhere to chill, crack open a classy red and watch the world go by. Non-members can book a table to gain entry. Membership £85

Crazy Larry's
533 Kings Rd, SW10 (entrance in Lots Rd)
(020) 7376 5555
Ⓤ Fulham Broadway
One of those places you just end up at. Nobody really knows why but everyone seems to leave safe in the knowledge that somewhere in the back of their mind, between the second and third shot of tequila, they had a good time. We are yet to meet Larry, or ascertain as to whether he is indeed, crazy. But with a club of this calibre to his name, we imagine he is. A fine example of Fulham at its least sophisticated and most fun.
Thu-Sat 10-2

Po Na Na Fez Club
222-224 Fulham Rd, SW1
(020) 7352 5978
Ⓤ Fulham B'way

Like Po Na Na's everywhere, a place to chill out amid Bedouin drapes and dim lighting. Pretend you're wearing a kaftan and hanging out with your fellow hippie souls in 1970s Morocco, or get the drinks in and dance to the funky mix of tunes. Po Na Na's is a pretty person magnet, if you don't leave with a handsome partner on your arm you'll at least have had fun looking.

fulham

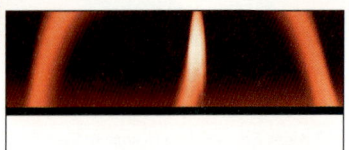

www.itchycity.co.uk

A famous Carnival, one of London's best markets and yeah, yeah that film. A few years back the Trinidadian community had the place pretty much to themselves, but now Notting Hill boasts more trendy celebs than your average album launch party. Not necessarily a good thing but Notting Hill remains a vibrant area with an unquestionable cool factor.

Bars

Beach Blanket Babylon
45 Ledbury Rd, W11 (020) 7229 2907
🚇 **Westbourne Park**

I went in here with the best intentions and ran out screaming. The place is full of estate agents trying to be hip, the bar-

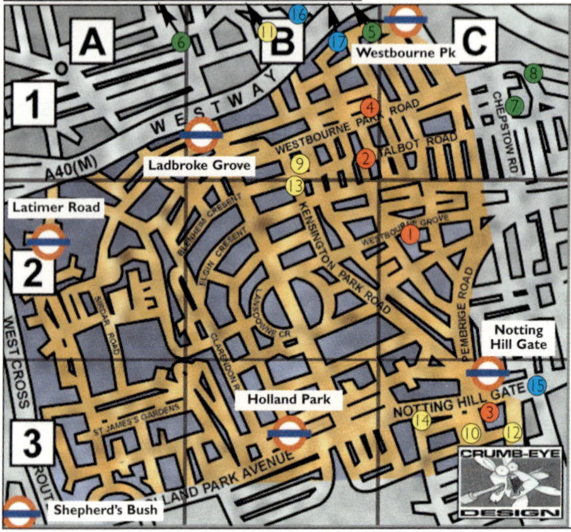

Bars
1. Beach Blanket Babylon
2. Coins
3. The Gate
4. Liquid Lounge

Pubs
5. The Golborne House
6. Paradise by way of Kensal Green
7. The Prince Bonaparte
8. The Westbourne

Restaurants
9. 192
10. Kensington Place
11. Ruby in the Dust
12. Sally Clarkes
13. Osteria Basilico
14. Pharmacy

Clubs
15. Notting Hill Arts Club
16. Subterania
17. Woody's

96 www.itchylondon.co.uk

staff look at you as though you've just fallen out of their nose, and after an hour of staring at the frenzied décor I became convinced I was about to be attacked by a gargoyle. All in all, highly distressing. Unless you want to buy a house.
Mon-Fri 12-11, Sat 11-11, Sun 11-10.30
Meal for two: £48 (Chateau Briand – beef dish to share)

Coins
105-107 Talbot Rd, W11
(020) 7221 8099 ⊖ **Ladbroke Grove**
East End café meets American diner. With its effortlessly beautiful clientele, gorgeously toned staff and madly hectic open kitchen, you'll be so enamoured with the sights, you could serve you an innersole and you'd be happy. But they won't. Coins is the place to go for breakfast and with its new licence, it's now the place to go for lunch, tea and dinner too.
Mon-Sat 8-4pm, Sun 8-5pm (recently stopped opening late, but set to start again by the summer)
Breakfast: £6.50 (comes highly recommended)

The Gate
87 Notting Hill Gate, W11
(020) 7727 9007 ⊖ **Notting Hill Gate**
Just like walking into an R&B video. Essentially a late night drinking hole with ultra-modern décor which belies its fairly benign reality. From Monday to Friday it's a good place to chill, but on weekends, we're talking serious crowds. With ultra-dim lighting, it's perfect for philanderers and ugly people. The food, however, is utterly fantastic.

Mon-Sat 5-1, Sun 5-12, Restaurant Mon-Sat 6-10.45, Sun 6-10.30
Meal for two: £36 (Grilled swordfish with udon noodles)

Liquid Lounge
209 Westbourne Park Rd, W11
(020) 7243 0914
⊖ **Ladbroke Grove/Westbourne Park**
Slip off your shoes and get horizontal in this incredibly chilled-out bar. With its deep blue walls, Antipodean staff and dark, leather booths, Liquid Lounge cries out for totally superficial conversations about your favourite tube lines: it's, like, totally West Coast, man. Not somewhere to go if you're on a bender and a bit loud.
Mon-Fri 5-12, Sat-Sun 10-12
Meal for two: £25 (Mussels with fries)

Pubs

The Golborne House
36 Golborne Rd, W10
(020) 8960 6260
⊖ **Westbourne Park or Ladbroke Gr.**
Just about the most perfect place for lounging your weekend away (apart from Jude Law's bed). The beautiful staff, sumptuous food and leather sofas mean you never have a reason to leave. Weeknights retain this chilled feel and are great for catching up on gossip and first dates – if you can keep your eyes off the bar staff.

Paradise...
...by way of Kensal Green
19 Kilburn Lane, W10 (020) 8969 0098
⊖ **Kensal Green (Bus: 52)**
A little way out lies the Paradise. The food and clientele are both nicely above average, but what you'll love is the décor. Deliciously dark downstairs, it invites all sorts of illicit naughtiness and furtive fumblings, while upstairs, wildly debauched dinner-parties can be held in one of the cosy private dining-rooms. All wonderfully Peter Greenaway. Exactly how pubs should be.

The Prince Bonaparte
80 Chepstow Rd, W2
(020) 7313 9491 ⊖ **Westbourne Park**
Once the dodgiest pub in Notting Hill, The Bonaparte recently enjoyed a bit of a revival with the likes of Stella McCartney calling it their local. Sadly this hey-day has gone and The Bonaparte is now a has-been with its trendy faces replaced by poncey media wannabes. The food's alright – if you can put up with the neighing 'ya's!' from the table next door.

The Westbourne
101 Westbourne Park Villas
W2 (020) 7221 1332
⊖ **Westbourne Park**
Pile on your labels and squeeze into this heaving pub alongside all the other Notting Hill posers; you'll find it about half a mile up it's own arse. A roped-in patio area contains the overspill from the bar, making the glam-crowd look like cattle in a holding pen. Smugly funny. Unfortunately, these people are painfully beautiful, so it may sound like bitterness to start taking the piss.

Restaurants

192
192 Kensington Park Rd, W11
(020) 7229 0482
⊖ **Ladbroke Grove/Notting Hill Gate**
For the times in your life when you just have to pose, head here. 192 holds the gold medal in ostentation – from its velvet boothed restaurant to its obnoxious, and often mad staff (my waiter barked like a dog). It also presents amazingly pre-

TOP FIVE...
Playing Pool
1. **Clerkenwell House (p115)**
2. **Elbow Rooms (p115/51)**
3. **Falcon (p84)**
4. **Arch 365 (p80)**
5. **Candy Bar (p110)**

tentious food – little things on weenie beds of green stuff with pine nuts, all piled up in the centre of huge white plates that taste good but are as filling as a rice-cake. No wonder everyone's so thin in there.
Mon-Fri 12.30-3 then 6.30-11, Sat 12.30-3.30 then 6.30-11, Sun 12.30-3.30 then 7-11. The bar is open throughout the day.
Meal for two: £36 (Roast sea bass with crab and vanilla)

Kensington Place
201-207 Kensington Church St, W8 (020) 7727 3184
◉ **Notting Hill Gate**
Apparently this was the late Princess Diana's favourite restaurant, and you can see why. Open plan, yet still maintaining a level of intimacy, you can sit and watch the well-heeled get well fed and well oiled. The food is exquisite, though thin on the vegetarian front. But with all of this comes a flip side – it's a bit too prim and proper to be much of a laugh. It needs a bit of a kicking to bring it down to earth.

Mon-Fri 12-3 then 6.30-11.45, Sat 12-3.30 then 6.30-11.45, Sun 12-3 then 6.30-10.15
Meal for two: £47 (Sea bass with citrus fruits and olive oil)

Ruby in the Dust
299 Portabello Rd, W11 (020) 8969 4626
◉ **Ladbroke Grove**
Ruby's is relaxed and cosy with a really good menu: a mix of Brit-dishes, Mexican offerings and enormous American brunches. And it all tastes fantastic. Unfortunately, the service doesn't. It's awful. Off-hand, and irritatingly slow, the waitresses wander around like post-lobotomy patients, struggling to remember what day it is. Intensely irritating.
Mon-Thu 11.30-11, Fri-Sun 10-11
Meal for two: £24 (Vegetarian sausages and mash)

you've tried this one...now try them all 17 other cities to indulge in

notting hill   99

Sally Clarkes

jamie oliver rates...

124 Kensington Church St, W8
(020) 7221 9225
🚇 **Notting Hill Gate**

Few places change their menu every week, but Sally's does, making it one of the most seasonal restaurants in the city. The food is a fusion of Italian and Californian, and there's a deli next door to pick up some of the ingredients. Spread over two floors, but if you can, bag a table downstairs and watch your tucker prepared in front of you. Top food and staff with warm personalities. Well recommended. J.O.

Meal for two: £44 pp for four courses. (Chargrilled loin of Roe deer)

Osteria Basilico

29 Kensington Park Rd, W11
(020) 7727 9372
🚇 **Ladbroke Grove/Notting Hill Gate**

One word: dough-balls. Snuggle into this gorgeously cosy restaurant and eat as many of them as you can; they are fantastic. Obviously save a little room for their pasta dishes, which are unusual and tasty. The relaxed, unpretentious atmosphere lends itself to noisy socialising and romantic rendezvous alike. Absolutely cracking.
Mon-Fri 12.30-3 then 6.30-11, Sat 12.30-4 then 6.30-11, Sun 12.30-3.15 then 6.30-10.30

Meal for two: £24 (Homemade pasta money bags with Parma ham)

Pharmacy

150 Notting Hill Gate, W11 (020) 7221 2442
🚇 **Notting Hill Gate**

Want to spend a stupid amount of money? Dine out at Damien Hirst's medicinal extravaganza. Mingle with the in-crowd on pill-shaped stools, necking cocktails from the narcotic-inspired list and picking at your plate of less than inspirational food. Sadly, it's only the amazing theme of this restaurant that really makes it worth the visit. That, and the thousands of branded drugs that line the walls, stirring up memories of past coughs and rashes. Hypochondriac heaven.
Mon-Thu 12-3 then 6-1, Fri-Sat 12-3 then 6-2, Sun 12-12

Meal for two: £50 (Roast leg of lamb)

Flick through the papers

Clubs

Notting Hill Arts Club

21 Notting Hill Gate, W11 (020) 7460 4459
🚇 **Notting Hill Gate**

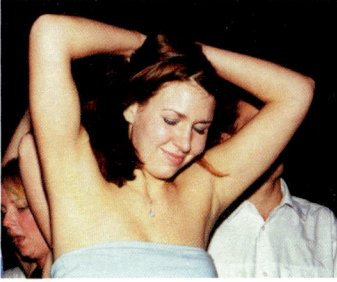

The only place in the entire world where you'll find Kate Moss rubbing shoulders with a 5ft2 Estonian foreign student in a bobble hat. The Arts Club is true Notting Hill and jam-packed with variety, from the aforementioned celeb/foreign students mix, to its ever changing club nights. Queuing's not even bad, thanks to the funky doorstaff – particularly the mad chick with red hair. Wednesday nights are legendary. In short – rock 'n'roll, baby, rock 'n'roll.

Subterania

36 Acklam Rd, W10 (020) 8960 4590
🚇 **Westbourne Park**

If you think you are/want Craig David, you'll fit in perfectly at Subterania. He met this girl on Monday, took her for a drink on Tuesday, they were making love by Wednesday. I reckon he needs to work on his technique. A big-ish underground club dedicated to R&B and swing, this place is wall-to-wall garage chic. Be prepared though, because honey, you're gonna sweat. And if you don't, you'll soon be covered in everyone else's. Delightful. Also, learn to blag because the queues are like Sainsbury's at Christmas. I opted for sexual favours. What would you do?

Woody's

41-43 Woodfield Rd, W9 (020) 7266 3030
🚇 **Notting Hill Gate**

Welcome to Notting Hell. Populated by drunken ex-public school types and other wannabes, this dull club is about as much fun as sawing your hand off with a blunt junior hacksaw. Woody's is pretentious, arsey and horribly sweaty. The music is uninspiring and the décor is forgettable. Which is sad, because Woody's once was something. Now it's merely somewhere.

RIZLA+ www.rizla.com

notting hill

out of our areas
www.itchycity.co.uk

If there's one thing that gets on our nerves, it's that London doesn't divide into handy book-sized areas. Here's the best and the worst of what didn't fit in anywhere else. For more reviews and stuff we couldn't even fit in here, check www.itchylondon.co.uk, part of a network of 18 itchycity sites.

Bars

Islington Bar
342 Caledonian Road, N1
(020) 7609 4917
⊖ **Caledonian Rd**

The Islington Bar used to be a wicked, local joint. The kinda place where at weekends it was a roadblock – turn up later than 10pm and you'd have either had to be the DJ, be shagging the DJ, or forget it. The place had a buzz. Sadly all this has changed. A new owner's moved in, along with his family of inept bar staff. The once-glorious bar has been transformed into some kind of sinister All Bar One come Turkish massage parlour hybrid. White-washed magnolia walls – check. Marble bar top – check. Faceless neon sign to replace trademark, wrought iron landmark – check. Hell, even the bar prices have gone up. What a freakin' disaster.
Mon-Wed 5-12, Thu-Fri 5-1, Sat 1.30-1, Sun 1.30-10.30. £3 after 9.30/8 Fri/Sat

Met Bar
Metropolitan Hotel, W1
(020) 7447 1000
⊖ **Hyde Park Corner**

Over-rated celebrity hangout – confirming that yes indeed pop stars have no idea

TOP FIVE...
Cheesy Tunes
1. **Strawberry Moons** (p16)
2. **Sound** (p42)
3. **Wessex House** (p87)
4. **Camden Palace** (p49)
5. **Limelight** (p42)

how to have a good time. Blagging your way past the bouncers requires fox-like cunning or seriously well-connected friends and once you're in you'll probably end up being forcibly ejected from your seat on account of the fact that Kavana has just entered the building. Non-members are welcome before six and if you look cool enough they might let you stay. Mon-Sun 11-6 (then it's member's only common people)

Ruby Lounge
33 Caledonian Rd, N1 (020) 7837 9558
Kings Cross

Ruby Lounge is a welcome haven amongst the sleaze of Kings Cross. Great cocktails, cool décor and deceptively comfortable looking seating. The days of waiting for your train in some dodgy pub amongst characters of ill-repute are over. What do you mean that's not necessarily a step forward?
Mon-Sat 12-11

Shoeless Joe's
Templace Place, Embankment
(020) 7240 7865
Embankment

I don't know why Joe hasn't got any footwear. You'd have thought that given how monied everyone is in this place, they could club together and sort him out. Victor Ubogu's ever-growing chain of plush bars are doing a roaring trade with their formula of bar come clubs come restaurant come sports screens galore. Beautiful crowds affecting devotions to teams they've never heard of pack the place out, and as the night draws on, the sport is replaced with roving cameras picking up glamorous people shots to project onto the walls. It shouldn't work, but it does.
Meal for two: 2 courses £15, House wine £11.50 (Pan-fried calf's liver)

Steam
Eastbourne Terrace, W2
Paddington

Opening any second now, in err, Paddington. Yes, yes we know it sounds dubious, Paddington ain't exactly the height of London cool. But this bar, set in an old railway hotel looks set to attract the crowds. We're talking cocktails and classy interiors. And hell, if it doesn't spearhead a revolution of bar culture in W2 it'll at least be one up on the Pride of Paddington.

Pubs

Bull's Head
15 Strand on the Green, W4
(020) 8994 1204
⊖ **Gunnersbury**

Ant and Dec's local. And aside the potential of sharing a bar stool with kids TV's golden boys it's a fine boozer. Riverside setting, great food and proper old pub interior. Cosy inside and equally equipped for outdoor drinking – just try and ignore the clatter of passing trains.

Queen Mary
Victoria Embankment, WC2
(020) 7240 9404
⊖ **Embankment**

A pub on a boat is a fine idea with endless comedy potential, except in winter when the novelty of outdoor drinking like pirates is replaced with a bog-standard pub interior, only made slightly nauseous by the swaying of the ship. Still, it's the finest place in London when the sun's shining.

Ship
41 Jew's Row, SW18 (020) 8870 9667
≋ **Wandsworth Town**

This is what summers' are made of. South London's pretty people lounging about on the outside picnic tables, a quality barbecue, the clinking of pint glasses, the shrill ring of mobile phones...

Trafalgar Tavern
Park Row, SE10 (020) 8858 2437
Docklands Light Rail: Cutty Sark

Massive pub with a fantastic view of the now defunct Dome. Live bands, outside seating, chilled riverside setting, it's as near as damn it perfect for summer piss ups. Attracts its fair share of tourists on account of some book that bloke Dickens penned here, not to mention the entirety of Goldsmith's College, but honestly, even if either of those points has just put you right off, it's a top boozer and plenty big enough for everyone.

TOP FIVE... Celeb Spotting
1. Red Cube (p36)
2. Sugar Reef (p14)
3. Stringfellow's (p33)
4. The Ivy (p30)
5. Joe Allen (p30)

Restaurants

Assaggi
jamie oliver rates...
39 Chepstow Place, W2
(020) 7792 5501
⊖ **Notting Hill Gate**

Honest, unpretentious, home-made Italian cooking. Sometimes the simple

things in life are the best, and that's certainly true of Assaggi. Plenty of people agree with me as well, because it's constantly packed out. Your best bet is to book well in advance to bag a table, but it's also worth chancing it on the day because you never know, someone may have cancelled. So informal you could get away with wearing your Bermudas, not that I would. J.O.

Mon-Sat 12.30-2, 7.30-9.30 (but open 'til 1am). Closed Sundays

Meal for two: £30 (Pecorino cheese with rocket and ham)

Fish!

Cathedral St, Borough Market, Southwark, SE1 (020) 7836 3236
London Bridge

Captain Birdseye would have a field day. Fish! offers just that, a startling array of freshly caught, lovingly prepared and distinctly edible marine life. They do have vegetarian and meat options, but this restaurant is understandably wasted on fish-phobics.

Mon-Fri 11.30-3, 5.30-11, Sat 5.30-11

Meal for two: £35 (Organic salmon)

Gordon Ramsay — jamie oliver rates...

68-69 Royal Hospital Road, SW3 (020) 7352 4441
Sloane Square

The public image of Gordon Ramsay as a miserable sod couldn't be further from the truth. The guy's a real comedian in the kitchen, providing you don't muck up. Ramsay shows how far French cooking has come in this country with a totally eclectic menu, a wonderful wine list and it's been rewarded with a third Michelin Star, the only place in London that can boast three of them. It's a bit pricey but if you really want to impress it's most definitely worth it. Make an effort on your appearance though or you might wind Gordon up — and you don't want to do that. J.O.

Mon-Fri 12-4, 6.45-11ish (later when busy).

Dinner menu: £75pp (Canon of lamb)

Monte's — jamie oliver rates...

164 Sloane St, SW1 (020) 7235 0555
Knightsbridge

OK, I might have more than a passing interest in this place as I'm one of the owners, but if you're looking to wine and dine in a relaxing and stylish environment then look no further. At lunchtime non-members are welcome, but if you're looking to get in for dinner, say you're interested in becoming a member and you'll get yourself a table — but you didn't hear that from me! The menu changes weekly, but always sticks to fusion Italian and English cuisine. Good, simple ingredients prepared by some top chefs, including myself. If you want to make a night of it you can go upstairs to the bar and try some of the cracking cocktails and then have a boogie

in the cheesy disco which stays open 'til 3. I'll see you on the dancefloor. J.O.
Mon-Sat 12-2, 6-3am (except Mon 'til 11 and Tue 'til 2)
Meal for two: £55 (Pot roasted wild duck)

Riva
jamie oliver rates...

169 Church Rd, SW13 (020) 8748 0434
≋ Barnes ⊖ Hammersmith
Another reason to leave the West End. They serve up an interesting selection of rural French cuisine, and consistently produce high quality grub. Reasonable prices and a laid-back atmosphere give it the thumbs up from me. J.O.
Mon-Fri 12-2.30, 7-11, Sat 7-11, Sun 12-2.30, 7-9.30
Meal for two: £45 (Partridge with chestnuts, shin of pork and pigs trotter)

River Café
jamie oliver rates...

Thames Wharf Rainville Rd, W6
(020) 7386 4200 ⊖ Hammersmith
No doubt you've already heard of it, and you've probably come across one of their many books by now, but if you haven't experienced the real deal then I suggest you get down there and sample it for yourself. The reasons for visiting are endless; the cool architecture, the best seasonal food anywhere, the extensive wine list, the service and the fact that relaxing by the river here is, without doubt, the best place to be in the summer. On top of all that they change the menu for every service, a nightmare for the chefs I can assure you, but great for the paying customer who can expect something different every time they turn up. Best to book, but worth turning up on the off chance. A cut above. J.O.
Mon-Sat 12.30-3, 7-9.30, Sun 12.30-3
Meal for two: £63 (Char-grilled sea bass)

Clubs

Po Na Na

230 Shepherds Bush Rd, W6
0800 783 7485 ⊖ Hammersmith
This spanking new Po Na Na is their most ambitious to date. The infamous 2230 capacity Hammersmith Palais has been converted into a shrine of North African exoticism. A main dance floor still remains, but they've also created secluded booths and intimate areas to keep the souk feel throughout. Fridays are funky, Saturdays more commercial. Recommended.

Ministry of Sound

103 Gaunt St (020) 7378 6528
⊖ Elephant & Castle
Super club extraordinaire attracting massive name DJs and an up for it crowd of weekend hedonists. It's the self appoint-

Hand book

ed home of house music and one of the few clubs in London where you'll still find girls in bikini tops and mini skirts going mental every weekend. The club's massive merchandising operation has helped take house to the high street.

Redbacks

264 High Street (020) 8896 1458
⊖ **Ealing Common/Acton Town**

This red-painted den of iniquity hides away in murky Acton. No dress code, no funny door policy, no posing, no looking cool, no sitting around the side of the bar, but you can be certain of huge queues, ridiculous tribute bands (Clouded House anyone?), and that the Antipodean crowd is completely and utterly pissed, up for a raging night out. Staggeringly brilliant and shocking in equal measures.

Rock

Victoria Embankment, WC2
(020) 7976 2006
⊖ **Charing Cross/Embankment**

Opulence, members bars and celebrity endorsement. Rock is Piers Adams newest project and definitely worth a look. Waterfalls, glitz and glamour transcends the divide between self-important posing joint and genuinely appealing place for a top night out. Music that gets the crowds on the dance floor and they refuse to let any one who used to be in Big Brother through the door. Get the champagne in and mingle with the best of them.

Scala

275 Pentonville Rd, N1
(020) 7833 2022 ⊖ **Kings Cross**

Kings Cross club set in an ex-theatre and host to some fine nights making it a popular choice with promoters, dance music insiders and people who plain as you like, know their stuff. No nasty door policies or dress codes, just quality house music and an appreciative crowd. You won't find the underage wonderbra and hot pants contingent in here.

Velvet Room

143a Charing Cross Rd, WC2
(020) 7734 4687
⊖ **Charing Cross/Embankment**

Sick of losing your mates and spending half the night in a queue for the cloakroom? A small venue, the antidote to superclubs, attracting big name DJs doing their thing and lots of hangers on. A truly excellent night out for anyone serious about their music. And right in the centre of London... who'd have thought it?

RIZLA+ It's what you make of it.

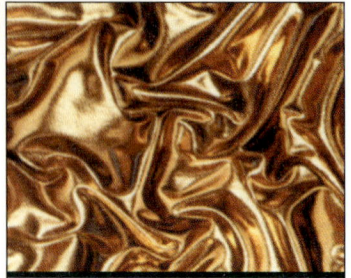

www.itchycity.co.uk

London's gay and lesbian scene is thriving and vibrant, centred mainly around the gay village of **Old Compton St**. With a barrage of gay bars and clubs and the majority of other trendy venues in the capital operating strict, gay-friendly policies there's somewhere on offer to suit any taste. Here's a taster.

Bars/Pubs

The Admiral Duncan
34 Old Compton St, W1
(020) 7437 5300
⊖ Tottenham Court Rd
Cinders and her staff will look after you in one of the oldest gay pubs in town. A good starting point for any night, with traditional pub décor and a mix of old and young. If Coronation St was in Soho this would be the Rovers.
Mon-Sat 12-11, Sun 12-10.30

Bar Aquda
13-14 Maiden Lane, WC2
(020) 7557 9891
⊖ Covent Garden
Definitely one to look out for. Admire the local art displays and friendly barmen while you tuck into some good pub grub. Holly Pennfield 'The Diva in the

Garden' appears once a month and the Mon-Thu happy hour (4-8) is worth a visit in itself.
Mon-Sat 12-11, Sun 12-10.30

Compton's of Soho
53-57 Old Compton St, W1
(020) 7479 7960
⊖ **Tottenham Court Rd**
Described by the popular gay press as a 'boots bar', that is, a lot of the guys are in denim and DMs. So if you fancy a pull that's as rough as their beard, you'd be wise to pop in. A circular bar means optimum cruising while you order your pint.
Mon-Sat 12-11, Sun 12-10.30

Freedom Café
60-66 Wardour St, W1 (020) 7734 0071
⊖ **Tottenham Court Rd/Piccadilly Circus**
A top choice for meeting up and losing an evening. Behind the facade of the innocent looking café bar is a steamy downstairs disco room. Upstairs café mochas and snacks are served 'til the early hours. Late licence, party atmosphere and we love the wall projections.
Mon-Sat 11-3, Sun 12-12 Admission £3 (Mon-Wed) £5 (Thu-Sat) after 11

Manto Café
30 Old Compton St, W1 (020) 7494 2756
⊖ **Tottenham Court Rd**
Its Manchester counterpart was made famous by Queer As Folk – but Soho's Manto has yet to receive the small screen treatment. Regardless, it's one of the most popular bars on the Compton strip and deservedly so. Can tend towards your overly style-conscious, fashion queens but then, this is Soho and it's much more fun that way.
Mon-Sat 11-12, Sun 11-10.30

Village Soho
81 Wardour St, W1 (020) 7434 2124
⊖ **Piccadilly Circus**
Good for drowning your sorrows when your latest conquest leaves you for something half your age and twice your looks. Go-go dancing and frisky customers make this a great venue for debauched weekends.
Mon-Sat 4-1, Sun 4-10.30

West Central
29-30 Lisle St, WC2 (020) 7474 7981
⊖ **Leicester Sq**
Very much an attitude free zone. The upstairs show bar guarantees a good night and cruising is at its optimum. The basement club gets hot but is worth the sweaty sheen. The only problem about this place is that it's hard to get in. Get there early to be sure.
Mon-Sat 3-3, Sun 3-10.30

Candy Bar

4 Carlisle St, W1 (020) 7494 4041
🚇 **Tottenham Court Rd**

Girls only and a world apart from any lesbian cliché you might care to consider. The best lesbian bar in London, stylish, trendy and packed to the rafters every night.
Mon-Thu 5-11.30, Fri-Sat 5-2, Sun 5-11.30 Admission £3/5 after 10 Fri/Sat

Clubs/Club nights

Heaven

Under the Arches, Craven Street, WC2
(020) 7930 2020
🚇 **Charing Cross**

An up for it, gay/mixed crowd make for a superb clubbing experience in this famed location near Charing Cross. Watch the hormones fly to a soundtrack of quality hard house. Friday nights display DJs and crowd at the peak of perfection – shine your halo and spruce up your wings – whether you like boys, girls, or a bit of both, everyone's an angel in Heaven

The Astoria

157 Charing Cross Rd, WC2
(020) 7434 0404
🚇 **Charing Cross**

The Astoria and its basement club LA2 offer some of London's campest gay nights. Maximum glitz attracts lip-synching, pop stars on singles promotion tours and the best-looking crowd around. Check out Fridays Camp Attack, Saturday's G.A.Y. and the rest of the week's cheaper offerings in LA2.

DTPM @ Fabric

77a CharterhouseSt (020) 7419 9199
🚇 **Farringdon**

Funky house and lots of posing at Fabric's Sunday night gay and lesbian extravaganza. Definitely the best place to end your weekend.

Popstarz @ the Scala

278 Pentonville Rd, N1 (020) 7738 9988
🚇 **Kings Cross**

Every taste catered for from house to disco, this popular Friday gay night attracts a friendly, lively crowd and the

Take a leaf out of our book

110

large helping of kitsch tack will keep the most discerning eighties band lover happy for hours. A perfect choice.

Trade @ Turnmills
Clerkenwell Rd, EC1 (020) 7250 3409
🚇 **Farringdon**
This long-running, hard house night (from 4am Saturdays) is still as popular as ever. Trade has built up an international name for itself over the last ten years and boasts a massive membership. You don't have to be a member, but to keep up on the gossip and get a discount on the door it'd be wise. A totally relaxed kind of vibe, this club is serious about its music.

Many other London clubs run excellent gay nights – check out itchylondon.co.uk for up to date details.

Shops and Services

24 hr Lesbian & Gay Switchboard
(020) 7837 7324

Chariots Roman Spa
201-207 Shoreditch High St, E1
(020) 7247 5333
🚇 **Liverpool St/Old St**
Massive gay sauna with a smaller branch on Cowcross St in Farringdon. Swimming pool, steam rooms, saunas and steamy goings on.

Freedom Cars
Gay cab service. See Getting About.

No.7 Guest House
7 Josephine Ave, SW2 (020) 8674 1880
A friendly gay hotel consistently receiving rave reviews. Breakfast is included.
£69 single/89 double (prices lower if you stay more than one night)

The Prowler Store
3-7 Brewer St, W1 (020) 7734 4031
🚇 **Tottenham Court Rd**
Stuck for something to buy your fag hag friends? Come on in for inspiration, stocking labels like Fred Perry and Diesel, mags, cards and ahem, novelty goods and videos. You won't be leaving empty handed.

RIZLA www.rizla.com

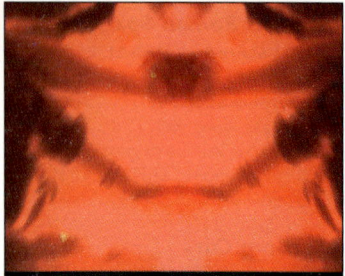

entertainment

www.itchycity.co.uk

Cinemas

Suffice to say, a cinema visit in the west end is going to be pricey. But, if you're central and fancy a bit of on-screen action, here are some of your options.

ABC Shaftesbury Ave
135 Shaftesbury Ave, WC2
0870 333 9067
⊖ **Leicester Sq**
2 screens.
£7.50, Mon-Tue-Thu before 5pm £5, NUS £5

ABC Piccadilly
215-217 Piccadilly, W1 0870 333 9067
⊖ **Piccadilly Circus**
3 screens.
£6, Mon and Tue-Fri before 5pm £4.30, NUS £4 (Tue-Fri only)

Curzon Soho
93-107 Shaftesbury Ave
(020) 7734 2255
⊖ **Leicester Sq**
Great for more unusual screenings, comfy seats, great bar and cheap food. Slightly disturbing healthy pick 'n' mix selection, but not enough to ruin your visit.
£8, Mon and Tue-Fri before 5pm £5, NUS £5 (Tue-Thu only)

The Metro Cinema
Rupert House, 19 Rupert St, W1
Info (020) 7437 0757
Booking (020) 7734 1506
⊖ **Leicester Sq**
Dodgy booking process in which a mumbling ansaphone man demands you leave your credit card details along with

a contact number in case there's a problem. Quite sinister. Some decent films though. £6.50, Mon and Tue-Fri before 5pm £4,

Odeon Leicester Square
40 Leicester Sq, WC2 0870 505 0007
🚇 **Leicester Sq**

Big blockbusters and premieres galore. £8.50-£10, Mon-Fri before 5pm £5-£6.50

Odeon Mezzanine
24-26 Leicester Sq, WC2 0870 505 0007
🚇 **Leicester Sq**
4 screens. All the big releases.
£7.50, Mon-Fri before 5pm £5

Prince Charles
7-10 Leicester Place, WC2 (020) 7734 9127
🚇 **Leicester Sq**
Cult, art house and general repertory flicks.

UGC Trocadero
Trocadero Centre, 13 Coventry St, W1
0870 9070712
🚇 **Piccadilly Circus**
£8.50, NUS Mon-Fri £6, Family tickets available.

The most skanky cinema in the west end, and you have to walk through a nightmare of arcade games and loitering youths to get there.

UCI Empire Leicester Square
5-6 Leicester Sq, WC2 0870 010 2030
🚇 **Leicester Sq**
£7.50-£9.50, Mon-Thur before 5pm £5-6

UGC Haymarket
63-65 Haymarket, SW1 0870 9070712
🚇 **Piccadilly Circus**
£8.50, NUS Mon-Fri £6, Family tickets available.

Warner Village West End
3 Cranbourn St, WC2
Info (020) 7437 4347
Booking (020) 7437 4343
🚇 **Leicester Sq**
£10, Mon-Fri before 7, NUS £7
Multi-screen, multi blockbusters.

★ THE INDEPENDENT   www.independent.co.uk

Away from the West End

Cut the cost of film going and watch the latest blockbuster somewhere local. Such venues are far too numerous to list, but every high street's got one. Check out www.itchylondon.co.uk. Tuesday nights are generally cut price.

The following cinemas are notable due to their penchant for festivals and artyness, which, if that's your thing...is good to know.

Barbican Screen
Silk St, Barbican, EC2 (020) 7382 7000
Moorgate/Barbican
£6.50, Members £5, NUS £4.50

Lux Cinema
2-4 Hoxton Square, N1 (020) 7684 0201
Old St

National Film Theatre
South Bank, Belvedere Rd, SE1
(020) 7633 0274
Waterloo

Riverside Studios Cinema
Crisp Rd, Hammersmith, W6
(020) 8237 1111
Hammersmith

The Vibe Bar
91-95 Brick Lane, E1 (020) 7426 0491
Aldgate East
Saturday Film Café, experimental and short films. Very east end cool.

Theatre

Stripping stars and Shakespearean seriousness - there are enough theatres in London to warrant an entire book just listing them and well, we don't have space for that. So, you can refer to our handy map if you know where you want to go, or www.itchylondon.co.uk for some pointers. Below are a few places to get your hands on some cheap tickets, without having to associate with bizarre characters in sandwich boards.

Stargreen Box Office
20 Argyll St, W1 (020) 7734 8932
Oxford Circus

The London Ticket Co
5-6 Leicester Sq, WC2 (020) 7434 1205
Leicester Sq
Sells cheap same-day tickets.

West End Theatre Bookings Ltd
Leicester Sq Stn, Charing Cross Rd, WC2
0845 1002002
Leicester Sq
Criterion Theatre, Piccadilly, W1
Piccadilly

Snooker/Pool Halls

Central London isn't exactly teaming with places to demonstrate how well you handle a cue...But if you're serious about a bit of hardcore practice before you start

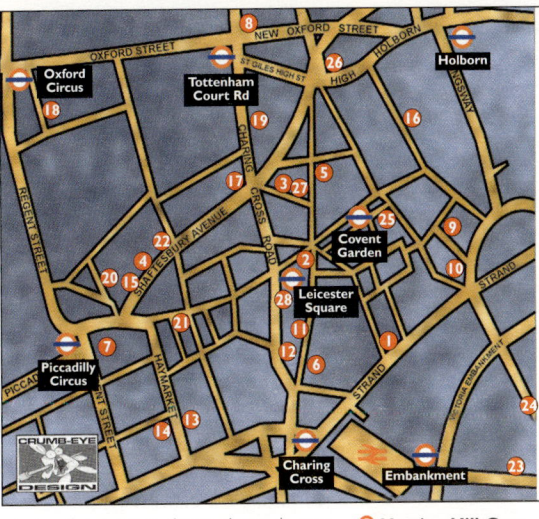

Theatres
1. Adelphi
2. Albery
3. Ambassadors
4. Apollo
5. Cambridge
6. Coliseum
7. Criterion
8. Dominion
9. Drury Lane Theatre
10. Duchess
11. Duke of Yorks
12. Garrick
13. Haymarket
14. Her Majesty's
15. Lyric
16. New London
17. Palace
18. Palladium
19. Phoenix
20. Piccadilly
21. Prince of Wales
22. Queens
23. Royal Festival Hall
24. Royal National
25. Royal Opera Hse
26. Shaftsbury
27. St. Martins
28. Wyndhams

playing for money down the pub, you might like to check out the following.

Brixton Snooker Centre
36-38 Acre Lane, SW2 (020) 7207 6762
🚇 Brixton

Camden Snooker Centre
16 Delancy St, NW1 (020) 7485 6094
🚇 Camden Town

Clerkenwell House
23-27 Hatton Wall, EC1 (020) 7404 1113
🚇 Chancery Lane/Farringdon
Bar/restaurant with a dedicated pool playing basement.

Elbow Room
103 Westbourne Grove, W2
(020) 7221 5211
🚇 Notting Hill Gate
89-91 Chapel Market, N1
(020) 7278 3244
🚇 Angel
Now we're talking. A pool hall/bar with decent music and great food. Plus you might even stand a chance of pulling. See Islington bar section.

entertainment   115

Riley's American Pool & Snooker Club
638-640 Wandsworth Rd, SW8
(020) 7498 0432
≷ **Wandsworth**
Open 24hrs Thu-Sat, 2am other times.

Suzy Q's
16 Semley Place, SW1 (020) 7824 8261
⊖ **Victoria**

Strip Joints

Now kids, we know those dodgy Soho strip-joints hold a certain appeal, but if you want something guaranteed (as much as we can) to be safe and free from scary rip-off scenarios you'd be wise to choose one of these to see a little lady action.

Astral
5 Brewer St, W1 (020) 7287 7988
⊖ **Piccadilly Circus**
Mon-Fri 8-2.30, Sat 9-2.30 (licensed 'til 3am)
Admission £15, £10 a dance (down to a g-string only)

Cabaret Of Angels
16-19 Upper St Martin's Lane, WC2
(020) 7240 5534
⊖ **Covent Garden**
Table dancing only, no disco anymore.
Mon-Sat 7.30-3
Admission £10 before 10, £15 after 10

The Lord Nelson
17 Mora St, EC1 (020) 7253 6389
⊖ **Old St**
This was used as a location in Lock Stock And Two Smoking Barrels.
Mon-Sun 11-11 No admission charge.

Raymond's Revue Bar
Walkers Court, W1 (020) 7734 1593
⊖ **Leicester Sq**
Erotica show at 8 and 10. Bar opens 7.30
Admission £10-25

Spearmint Rhino's
161 Tottenham Court Rd, W1
(020) 7209 4488
⊖ **Tottenham Court Rd**
Mon-Sat 11am-2, Sun 12-12
Admission £10 before 11, £15 after

Art

National Gallery
Trafalgar Sq, WC2 (020) 7839 3321
⊖ **Trafalgar Sq**
Exhaustingly enormous array of paintings. Guaranteed to give you 'I can't handle looking at any more' type anxiety within the hour.
Mon-Sun 10-6 Admission free

National Portrait Gallery
St Martin's Place, WC2 (020) 7306 0055
⊖ **Trafalgar Sq**
Portraits in chronological order from

middle ages to present day.
Mon-Wed 10-6, Thu-Fri 10-9, Sat 10-6, Sun 12-6 Admission free

Saatchi Gallery
98a Boundary Rd, NW8 (020) 7624 8299
🚇 **Kilburn Park**
The car showroom of the art world.
Thu-Sun 12-6 Admission £4/2

The Serpentine Gallery
Hyde Park (020) 7402 6075
🚇 **Hyde Park Corner**
A day out in itself. Beautiful location and contemporary displays.
Mon-Sun 10-6 Admission free

Tate Britain
Millbank, SW1 (020) 7887 8000
🚇 **Pimlico**
Archive of British art, all the pre-Tate Modern stuff.
Mon-Sun 10-5.50 Admission free

Tate Modern
Queen's Walk, SE1 (020) 7887 8000
🚇 **Blackfriars/London Bridge**
Set in a former power station, this impressive building is home to the best in 20th century and modern art. A definite must-see.
Mon-Sun 10-5.50 Admission free

White Cube
Hoxton Square
🚇 **Old St**
Hip, Brit-art gallery featuring the likes of Tracey Emin.

Comedy

Comedy Café
66 Rivington St, EC2 (020) 7739 5706
🚇 **Old St**

Comedy Store
**Haymarket, 1a Oxendon St, SW1
(020) 7344 0234**
🚇 **Piccadilly Circus**

Jongleurs
Battersea, The Cornet, 49 Lavender Gardens, SW11 (020) 7564 2500
🚇 **Clapham Junction**
Camden Lock, Dingwalls Building, Middle Yard, Camden Lock, Camden High St, NW1 (020) 7564 2500
🚇 **Camden Town**
**Bow Wharf, 221 Grove Rd, E3
(020) 7564 2500**
🚇 **Mile End**
For more, see www.itchylondon.co.uk

Museums

British Museum
Great Russell St, WC1 (020) 7636 1555
🚇 **Tottenham Court Rd**
Massive museum housing all manner of

old things from copper Buddhas to 16th century ship clocks.
Mon-Wed 10-5.30, Thu-Fri 10-8.30, Sat 10-5.30, Admission free

Design Museum
28 Shad Thames, SE1 (020) 7403 6933
🚇 **Tower Hill**
A celebration of product design and shop that you'll actually want to buy things from.
Mon-Fri 11.30-6, Sat-Sun 10.30-6
Admission £5.50/£4.50 NUS

London Dungeon
28-34 Tooley St, SE1 (020) 7403 7221
🚇 **London Bridge**
Gory exhibits and actors in various stages of death. Even the 'kids of today' will love it.
Mon-Sun 10-5 (open until 8 peak season) Admission £10.95/£9.50 NUS

London Transport Museum
Covent Garden Piazza, WC2
(020) 7565 7299
🚇 **Covent Garden**
A trip to the London Transport Museum is genuinely not as boring as you might expect. London's public transport (the oldest in the world) comes to life with interactive displays and simulators.
Mon-Thu 10-6, Fri 11-6, Sat-Sun 10-6
Admission £5.50/£2.95 conc.

Madame Tussaud's
Marylebone Rd, NW1 (020) 7935 6861
🚇 **Baker St**
Ah, the comedy potential. Sidle up to a wax Kylie and get your picture taken. Beware mammoth queues.
Mon-Sun 10-5.30 Admission £11.95

Millennium Dome
Oh woe to London citizens. The shameful waste of public funds has left behind this empty shell in the middle of Greenwich. The trapeze artists have moved on, and all we're left with is an impressive looking car park.

Natural History Museum
Cromwell Rd, SW7 (020) 7938 9123
🚇 **South Kensington**
Self explanatory really. Stuffed dead animals and dinosaurs bones. Not enough buttons to press for our liking.
Mon-Sat 10-5.50, Sun 11-5.50 Admission £7.50/£4.50 NUS

Victoria & Albert Museum
Cromwell Rd, SW7 (020) 7938 8500
🚇 **South Kensington**
Sorry to be uncultured and down right disrespectful, but there really are better ways to spend a Sunday afternoon.
Mon-Sat 10-5.50, Sun 11-5.50 Admission £6/free NUS

Tourist Attractions

Ok, so you're a tourist and you're in London. What you're going to need is a handy top-ten...well look no further. Tick at least five off, even if you just see them from a distance and you'll have more sights under your belt than the average Londoner.

1. Big Ben/Houses of Parliament (⊖ Westminster)
2. St Paul's Cathedral (⊖ St Paul's)
3. Hyde Park (⊖ Hyde Park Corner)
4. Buckingham Palace (⊖ St James Park)
5. Tower Bridge (⊖ Tower Hill)
6. Tower of London, crown jewels, ravens, towers and the like. (⊖ Tower Hill)
7. Millennium Wheel, giant fairground attraction (⊖ Waterloo)

8. Little Venice (⊖ Warwick Avenue)
9. Westminster Abbey (Dean's Yard, SW1 ⊖ Westminster)
10. No.10, Tony actually lives at No.11 (⊖ Westminster)

Alternative Attractions

1. Abbey Rd Studios, go on, do the zebra crossing thing, hold up traffic, everyone else does.
(3 Abbey Rd, NW8 ⊖ St Johns Wood)
2. Blind Beggar, legendary east end boozer, famed as the site of Ronnie Kray's 1966 fatal shooting of George Cornell. Rumour has it you can still see the bullet holes.
(337 Whitechapel Rd, E1 ⊖ Whitechapel)
3. Primrose Hill, a stunning view of London and jogging ground for the local residents, Jude, Sadie et al.
(⊖ Chalk Farm/St John's Wood)
4. Highgate Cemetery, Karl Marx is buried here, pay homage.
(⊖ Highgate)
5. There's always that massive glass fronted Tesco's in Kensington.

Casinos

By law, applications must be made 24 hours in advance.

Grosvenor Casino
Victoria, 150-162 Edgware Rd
(020) 7262 7777
⊖ Edgware Rd
The Gloucester, 4-18 Harrington Gardens (020) 7373 7134
⊖ Gloucester Rd

Ladbroke Casino Piccadilly
196 Piccadilly (020) 7534 7600
⊖ Piccadilly Circus

London Clubs Casino
Knightsbridge, Mayfair (x3) and Soho. Ring 07000 707 606 for details

Discover 200 years of history at London's Transport Museum.

Buses, trams and trains
Changing exhibitions
Interactive displays
Tube simulators
KidZones ♦ Funbus
Shop & cafe

Now

Open daily 10.00 - 18.00
(Fridays 11.00 - 18.00)

London's Transport Museum
Covent Garden Piazza

Events and times vary.
For details telephone
(020) 7565 7299
or visit our Web site at
www.ltmuseum.co.uk

24 hr London

1997
19 Wardour St (020) 7734 2868
🚇 Leicester Sq/Tottenham Court Rd
Chinese café.

Bar Italia
22 Frith St, W1 (020) 7437 4520
🚇 Leicester Sq
Probably London's most popular 24hr café and hangout for future artists and musicians. Now only open 24hr Fri/Sat.

Bonafide Studios
Unit B-B2, Burbage House, 83-85
Curtain Rd, EC2 (020) 7684 5350
🚇 Old St
You know that 4am feeling where you just have to lay down that new track?

Brick Lane Beigel Bake
159 Brick Lane, E1 (020) 7729 0616
🚇 Aldgate East/Liverpool St
The best bagels in town.

Café Boheme
13-17 Old Compton St, W1
(020) 7734 0623
🚇 Leicester Sq
Open 24hrs Fridays and Saturdays.

---

great gaming

GROSVENOR CASINOS

starts here

Restaurant & Bars Open 7 Days a Week

4 casinos to choose from

For **FREE** membership call FREEPHONE 08080 21 21 21

The Connoisseur Club
London Park Tower
The Gloucester Casino
The Grosvenor Victoria

Open 2pm - 4am daily

Roulette Blackjack
Casino Stud Poker
Dice Cardroom
Punto Banco
Jackpot Machines

Please check individual casinos for gaming facilities

24 hours must elapse between receipt of application and participation in gaming.
Members must be aged 18 years and over.

entertainment

121

EasyEverything
358 Oxford St, W1
🚇 **Bond St**
9-16 Tottenham Court Rd
🚇 **Tottenham Court Rd**
24hr internet access – cheaper the more ludicrous the hour of the day.

Joe's Basement
113 Wardour St (020) 7439 3210
🚇 **Leicester Sq/Tottenham Court Rd**
Photographic supplies and developing.

Stepney Snooker Club
137a Whitehorse Rd, E1 (020) 7790 9569
🚇 **Stepney Green**

Tinseltown
44-46 St John St, EC1 (020) 7689 2424
🚇 **Farringdon**
24 hr menu feeding the work-all-night dot com kids in the area.

Vingt Quatre
325 Fulham Rd, SW10 (020) 7376 7224
🚇 **Fulham Broadway**
Over-priced nosh, round the clock.

Sport

Football

Arsenal Football Club
Highbury, Avenell Rd, N5 (020) 7704 4000
🚇 **Arsenal**
London's most successful team, and still the best. Worth checking out the marble halls of Highbury, if you haven't already, before they move to a bigger stadium.

Charlton Athletic Football Club
The Valley, Floyd Rd, SE7 (020) 8333 4010
🚆 **Charlton Rd**
After years of ground sharing with Crystal Palace, Charlton are now back at the Valley. Expect manager Alan Curbishley to be poached by one of the big boys very soon.

Chelsea Football Club
Stamford Bridge, Fulham Rd, SW6 (020) 7385 5545
🚇 **Fulham Broadway**
You either love 'em or hate 'em. Rub shoulders with celebrities and politicians, if you can afford the astronomical ticket prices.

Tottenham Hotspur
White Hart Lane, 748 High Rd, N17 (020) 8365 5000
🚆 **White Hart Lane**
The glory, glory days disappeared from White Hart Lane a long time ago, and aren't on the brink of return... yet.

West Ham United
Upton Park, Green St, E13 (020) 8548 2748
🚇 **Upton Park**

Hammers fans will gladly tell you how 'they' won the World Cup in 1966, supplying Moore, Hurst and Peters to the team, but that's about all they have won.

Other grounds

Cheaper tickets available for the likes of Leyton Orient, Barnet, Millwall or Brentford, but don't expect to see much quality. For a slightly higher standard you could visit Fulham, Queens Park Rangers, Wimbledon, Crystal Palace or Watford, all recently Premiership clubs, but without any Premiership stars nowadays.

Cricket

London can boast two of the finest test grounds in the country. If only we could boast one of the world's finest international teams. The atmosphere at Lords and the Oval is a bit more restrained than up north but it's still a good crack.

Lord's
St John's Wood Rd, NW8 (020) 7289 1611
 St John's Wood

Oval
Kennington Oval, SE11 (020) 7582 6660
 Oval

Rugby Union

Twickenham
Rugby House, 21 Rugby Rd
(020) 8892 2000
🚆 **Twickenham**

Hugely impressive after its redevelopment. Unlike football supporters, rugby fans can get blind drunk and not cause trouble. In fact it's the law that when you go to an international match that you must get slaughtered, as the England team usually do to the opposition on the pitch.

Tennis

Wimbledon
All England Lawn Tennis Club, Church Rd, SW19 (020) 8944 1066
 Southfields/Wimbledon Park

Outrageously expensive strawberries and cream, champagne and bus loads of the middle-classes scrambling to get a good seat on Court 38.

The Dogs

Walthamstow
Chingford Rd, E4 (020) 8531 4255
🚇 **Walthamstow Central**

Legendary venue for watching the dogs, and still massively popular. You can make a real night of it, have a meal, and watch from the comfort of your table, but you'll have to book early as half the population of the East End seems to be there.

123

entertainment

shopping
www.itchycity.co.uk

London's shopping possibilities are endless and an entire tourist attraction in themselves. Obviously we can't feature anywhere near everything here, but this little lot should give you something to go on.

When to shop
Shop opening times are generally:
Mon-Wed 10-7
Thu 10-8
Fri-Sat 10-7
Sun 12-6

Shopping Areas

Carnaby St
⊖ Oxford Circus

Carnaby St was cool in the sixties, which means the Beatles must have walked down it at least once, which means eighteen year old Japanese students are obliged by law to flock in their thousands. There's a fair bit for them to flock for. A great trainer shop, Diesel, Mikey, Soccer Scene and all the novelty key rings and platform boots they could ask for.

Covent Garden/Neal St
⊖ Covent Garden

It's easy to get very cynical about the intelligence level of your average international visitor after an afternoon here, but get over it because some of the city's finest designer boutiques are all within walking distance of one another, offering everything from Pepe to Paul Smith, bargain independent outlets and a tacky market to boot. Crowds aside, it's easy to find what you want.

C O R K E R

For the full Rizlaware range just visit www.rizla.com or call 07000 749527

High St Kensington
🚇 **High St Kensington**

Everything you'd expect from a London high street and good when you'd rather eat your own head than set foot in Oxford Street. You'll find Hennes, a big department store and most notably, Urban Outfitters, an Americana-arama selling cool clothes and trendy homewares.

Kings Rd
🚇 **Sloane Square**

Its 1960's kudos is long gone but the shops remain. A fairly uninspiring place to do the Saturday shopping thing but a damned sight less crowded than your other options. Sloaney boys and girls in pashminas, posh folks supermarket Waitrose and a damned good Oxfam full of the aforementioneds' worn once cast-offs.

Oxford St
🚇 **Oxford Circus**

A shopping Mecca enjoying a renaissance of cool. Major chains compete for the best flagships, and market geezers flog plastic handbags and 'My mate went to London and all I got was this lousy t-shirt' t-shirts. Terminally crowded, inducing panic attacks, insanity and murderous tendencies in the calmest of shoppers. Breathe deeply and forget the concept of personal space.

New Bond St/Old Bond St/South Molton St
🚇 **Green Park/Bond St**

Trust fund? Lottery winnings? New gold card? That's you lot out then. The place to come for serious spending. Mess up the displays in Browns, try to look like you belong in Prada, and tuck into an Egg McMuffin outside Tiffany's. Darling, nowhere else in London will do.

Sloane St
🚇 **Knightsbridge**

Designer old timers from Chanel to Gucci. Fun to look at, enter if you dare.

Department Stores

Debenhams
334-348 Oxford St, W1 (020) 7408 4444
🚇 **Bond St/Oxford Circus**

The designers at Debenhams range makes this once average department store well worth a mention. The likes of John Rocha and Pierce Fionda have cre-

ated one-off collections for men and women, at normal person prices, with fantastic results. Perfect for wannabe film stars, special occasions or just trying on.
Mon-Tue 9.30-7, Wed 10-8, Thu-Fri 9.30-8, Sat 9-7, Sun 12-6

Harrods
Knightsbridge, SW1 (020) 7730 1234
Knightsbridge
Visitors to Harrods fall into two categories. The kind who've realised through long-standing richness and detachment from reality, that you are nothing until you own a gold toothpick, and the kind who buy a novelty pencil just so they can get their hands on a carrier bag. No in-betweens. An essential (if you really must) stop-off. And flashing your passport at Mohammed is not considered appropriate behaviour.
Mon-Tue 10-6, Wed-Fri 10-7, Sat 10-6

Harvey Nichols
109-125 Knightsbridge, SW1
(020) 7235 5000
Knightsbridge
Browsing ground only, for most of us anyway. Admire straight off the catwalk fashion and sink a few spritzers in the fifth floor bar. Full of loud, important people shouting into mobile phones, and heavily made-up ladies who don't lunch because food is too last season.
Mon-Tue 10-6, Wed-Fri 10-8, Wed 10-8, Thu-Sat 10-7, Sun 12-6

John Lewis
278-306 Oxford St, W1 (020) 7629 7711
Oxford Circus
Fairly average, but reliable store stocking everything you'd expect; fashion, shoes, cosmetics and a particularly good household and electrical section. Hours of fun browsing teapots and microwaves. Oh yes.
Mon-Wed 9.30-6, Thu 10-8, Fri 9.30-6, Sat 9-6

Selfridges
400 Oxford St, W1 (020) 7629 1234
Bond St
An enormous, ornate building and a must visit for any serious shopper. High street fashion, designer everything, tights, toasters – whatever you're into, you'll find it here, eventually. You're guaranteed to leave poorer but the convenient

indoor amble between retailers makes up for it. One stop shopping – go departmental.
Mon-Wed 10-7, Thu-Fri 10-8, Sat 10-7, Sun 12-6

Markets

Brick Lane
🚇 **Aldgate East**
In the very heart of London's Bangladeshi community. Brick Lane is the best place to come for some real east end feeling. Jellied eels and knocked off bikes a plenty.
Sun 8-1

Camden Market
🚇 **Camden Town**
London's biggest market attraction manages to get by despite offering little more than a load of old tat. Everything costs a seemingly obligatory twenty pounds and because you're at a market you think it's a bargain. Remember, Camden Town is exit only at peak market times so you'll have to walk to Mornington Crescent or Chalk Farm to escape the madness.
Sat-Sun 10-6

Columbia Rd Flower Market
🚇 **Shoreditch**
Word on the street is that the east end is a bit cool. Soaking it all up at this Sunday morning bartering institution has to be one of the best ways to spend your hangover time. Kerb to kerb flowers and brilliant stallholder banter. Stop off for a fry-up in the bizarrely Mexican themed café above The Royal Oak, or try some cockles from Lee's Seafood's.
Sun 8-1

Petticoat Lane
🚇 **Liverpool St**
Patsy Palmer's favourite east end market, or so we hear. There's certainly nothing hip about Petticoat Lane, in fact it's as near to the Albert Square bench mark as you'll get. Tacky sunglasses and dodgy leggings galore.
Sun 9-2

Portobello
🚇 **Notting Hill Gate/Ladbroke Grove**
Hugh Grant has got a lot to answer for. Notting Hill's box-office success (yes, you'll find the house on Westbourne Grove) means everyone wants a bit of

Portobello. The market remains one of London's best. Antiques, flowers, fruit and veg and the best up and coming young designer clothes. If you want to stand out from the crowd in a second hand Afghan or be there first before Vogue get their hands on fresh fashion blood you're in the right place. Fridays for fashion. Saturdays for antiques.
Open daily

Spitalfields
 Liverpool St

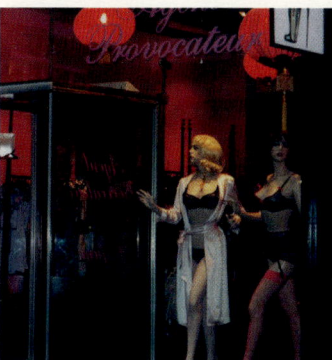

Perfect for those weird and wacky but utterly useless Christmas presents and deconstruction t-shirts you wear once then wonder what on earth possessed you. A food-fest too, with home made cake stands, Thai, jacket spuds, Chinese, pancakes and falafels. Definitely ranks alongside Portobello although sadly smack bang in the middle of City development plans. Don't worry, by the time you've wandered round all afternoon you'll be a comrade in the save old markets committee, wearing a 4th hand sheepskin coat, with braided hair and a rejuvenated karma.
Open daily but best on Sat/Sun

Women's Fashion

Agent Provocateur
6 Broadwick St, W1 (020) 7439 0229
Leicester Sq

Risque and reassuringly expensive (Kate Moss shops here don't you know) underwear. Appealing to boys and girls, but for different reasons. Check out the impressive window displays then make a bee-line for their considerably cheaper, diffusion line in M&S.

Mango
Regent St, W1 (020) 7434 1384
Piccadilly Circus

Spanish label delivering top quality, low price fashion. Unusual finds and catwalk copies. If you're just here for the weekend, make the trip.

Miss Sixty
Neal St, WC2 (020) 7836 3789
Covent Garden

Cute, casual clothes for modern day sixties chicks.

Zara
118 Regent St, W1 (020) 7534 9500
Piccadilly Circus

Likewise senoritas. Another rock-bottom price range, Spanish shop throwing Espana in the works for your traditional fashion chains. Great for tall, model types and short, ugly people with sewing machines.

shopping 129

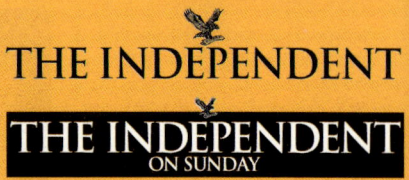

why not subscribe and

save over 60%

For a limited period only, The Independent would like to offer you the chance to purchase The Independent & Independent on Sunday for only £1.50 a week, with our advanced purchase payment subscription. Payments can be made by simply telephoning

0800 783 1920

quoting REFERENCE IS01000ITCHY

Offices open Mon to Fri 9am - 9pm, Sat & Sun 10am - 4pm

Answer machine at all other times.

When the application has been processed - which may take up to three weeks - The Independent will send you your fully pre-paid vouchers, which can be redeemed at any news outlet. Alternatively, if you prefer home delivery, please let us know the details of your local participating newsagent (including address and postcode) and we can organise the rest! Your newsagent may charge a nominal fee for this service.

Unisex Fashion

Diesel
43 Earlham St, WC2 (020) 7379 4660
- Covent Garden

Super trendy and ever popular jeans and casual wear.

Red or Dead
41-43 Neal St, WC2 (020) 7379 7571
- Covent Garden

Wacky, youthful fashion and bags and shoes that fall apart on the second wear. Well mine always do anyway.

Urban Outfitters
36-38 High St Kensington, W8
(020) 7761 1001
- High St Kensington

Come out of the tube, turn right and walk to the top of the high street. We know it sounds unlikely but you are now entering a rare example of something good that has come out of America. Great clothes, gift ideas and cool household stuff to look out of place in your dodgy but cheap council flat.

TopShop/TopMan
214 Oxford St, W1 (020) 7636 7700
- Oxford Circus

If you could take one thing with you to a desert island it should be this. A shopping Bermuda triangle, offering everything that anyone could ever need. Frankly, I'd happily move in, if only they'd let me.

Nike Town
236 Oxford St, W1 (020) 7761 1001
- Oxford Circus

Nike may well be the devil's work in the eyes of the world's fair trading crusaders but it doesn't seem to have affected their sales figures. Not if this enormous extravaganza of Nike-ness is to be taken into consideration. All very hi-tech and dauntingly big.

Men's

Duffer of St George
29 Shorts Gardens, WC2
(020) 7379 4660
- Covent Garden

Remains the cool boy about town's favourite for clothes. Casual chic at not entirely casual prices.

Boxfresh
2 Shorts Gardens, WC2 (020) 7240 4742
⊖ Covent Garden
Recently started a line for women but still mainly one for the boys. Stylish fashion.

Jigsaw Menswear
Floral St, WC2 (020) 7240 5651
⊖ Covent Garden
Boring but nice clothes for boys who've grown out of Top Man.

Second Hand

Oxfam Originals
26 Ganton St, W1 (020) 7437 7338
⊖ Oxford Circus
To save you sorting through dodgy tracksuits, Oxfam Originals cuts it down to the stuff worth having. So, retro sixties and seventies gear and other great finds at walk out of the shop prices.

Pop Boutique
6 Monmouth St, WC2 (020) 7497 5262
⊖ Covent Garden
A rainbow of second hand bargains.

Yesterday's Bread
29-31 Foubert's Place, W1
(020) 7287 1929
⊖ Oxford Circus

Headache inducing facade and hippie nostalgia within. A great place for one-off t-shirts and accessories, and for boring people who've decided to start expressing their unconventional side.

Designer

Browns
23-27 South Molton St, W1
(020) 74917833
⊖ Bond St

A massive array of designer clothes and accessories at intimidating prices, with equally intimidating staff. Probably best to talk loudly about your new record deal and last nights date with Tara P-T, if you're not dripping in gold.

Gucci
18 Sloane St, SW1 (020) 7235 6707
⊖ Knightsbridge
33 Old Bond St, W1 (020) 7629 2716
⊖ Green Park
I always like to call ahead to make sure I won't have to share changing space with any common folk. You should probably do the same.

soletrader

the ultimate range of designer and branded footwear

72 Neal St. Covent Garden, London. Tel: 020 7836 6777
&
96A Kensington High St. London. Tel: 020 7361 1560

Joseph
23 Old Bond St, W1 (020) 7629 3713
⊖ **Bond St**

A selection of designer threads and a good own label, which is not totally inaccessible price wise. Having said that it's still bloody expensive – send a guilt-ridden, absentee parent with a shopping list.

Paul Smith
40-44 Floral St, WC2 (020) 7379 7133
⊖ **Covent Garden**

Brit boy done good with popular fashion for man, woman and child.

Designer Discount

Browns Labels for Less
50 South Molton St, W1 (020) 7514 0052
⊖ **Bond St**

The stuff London's It boys and girls didn't want, at discount prices.

Joseph Sale Shop
53 King's Rd, SW3 (020) 7730 7562
⊖ **Sloane Sq**

Smith Sale Shop
23 Avery Row, W1 (020) 7493 1287
⊖ **Bond St**

Paul Smith for less.

Shoes

Buffalo
47-49 Neal St, WC2 (020) 7379 1051
⊖ **Covent Garden**

Old school Spice shoes. Ridiculous platforms and sky high trainers for boys and girls who don't trip over.

Offspring
60 Neal St, WC2 (020) 7497 2463
⊖ **Covent Garden**

You can tell a lot about a person by their choice of trainer. Make sure yours give the right impression with this startling array.

soletrader
72 Neal Street, Covent Garden
(020) 7836 6777 ⊖ **Covent Garden**
96A Kensington High Street
(020) 7361 1560 ⊖ **High St. Kensington**

With a shockingly large collection of both mainstream brands (Nike, Adidas, Puma etc) and funkier ones (Diesel, FCUK, Converse and what have you), to be brutally honest, if you can't find the footwear you need here, you probably aren't even looking for shoes.

GOJOBSITE™

THIS BOOK HAS THE BEST PLACES TO SPEND YOUR MONEY.

WE HAVE THE BEST PLACES TO MAKE MORE MONEY.

We have hundreds of thousands of new jobs every month from Europe's leading companies. You could find your dream job in seconds, and you might soon need an Itchy Guide to New York, Paris, Sydney…

www.gojobsite.co.uk

Music

Ambient Soho
4 Berwick St, W1 (020) 7437 0521
🚇 **Oxford Circus/Tottenham Court Rd**
Dance specialists covering every genre known to man, and a few more which I'm sure have just been made up by the staff. Heaven for all those ravers out there who refuse to believe that 1988 ever ended.

Atlas
11 Archer St, W1 (020) 7494 0792
🚇 **Piccadilly Circus**
Electronica experts, and placed handily for a quick look round the sex shops. Full of rare cuts by Croatian DJs and the like, as well as some closer to home, but thankfully not overrun with staff who refuse to acknowledge you unless you boast an encyclopaedic knowledge of the New York underground scene.

Black Market Records
25 D'Arblay St W1 (020) 7287 1932
🚇 **Oxford Circus/Tottenham Court Rd**
Popular with the kids, especially on Saturdays, and if you can put up with that then you'll find it's one of the best

Books

Foyle's
113-119 Charing Cross Rd, WC2
(020) 7437 5660
🚇 **Tottenham Court Rd**
A massive, baffling array of reading material, old, new and discontinued.

Helter Skelter
4 Denmark St (020) 7836 1151
🚇 **Tottenham Court Rd**
An entire shop dedicated to books about popular music. Row upon row of rock biographies and no dull accounts of Mozart's early years. Hurrah

Waterstone's
203-206 Piccadilly, W1 (020) 7851 2400
🚇 **Piccadilly Circus**
The latest and largest from the chain, and this one's got a licensed bar as well. Far more civilised to choose between Geri Halliwell's If Only and The Complete Works of Shakespeare over a couple of glasses of wine, don't you think?

shopping

stocked shops for underground house, garage, hardcore and jungle.

HMV
150 Oxford St, W1 (020) 7631 3423
🚇 **Oxford Circus**
Very big, very busy and very well stocked.

Mister CD
80 Berwick St, W1 (020) 7439 1097
🚇 **Oxford Circus/Tottenham Court Rd**
I can still recall the moment of joy when I first came across this little goldmine. Yeah, alright, I don't get out much, but where else in the centre of London can you find new release CDs for a tenner or less? He's a diamond geezer Mister CD.

Reckless Records
30 Berwick St, W1 (020) 7437 4271
🚇 **Oxford Circus/Tottenham Court Rd**
Huge selection of second hand vinyl and CDs, specialising in indie and rock. It can be a bit of a chore fighting it out in the tight spaces. Not something which is likely to bother the committed record buyer though.

Sister Ray
94 Berwick St, W1 (020) 7287 8385
Immortalised on the cover of Oasis' (What's The Story) Morning Glory? album sleeve, Berwick St. is home to some of London's finest record shops, Sister Ray being one of those. Cheap, strictly independent with knowledgeable staff.

Tower Records
1 Piccadilly Circus, W1 020 7439 2500
🚇 **Piccadilly Circus**
Slap bang on the corner of one of London's busiest areas. Expect to find lots of European and Japanese tourists oohing and ahhing over the latest homegrown talent from Dudley.

Virgin Megastore
Oxford St, W1 (020) 7631 1234
🚇 **Tottenham Court Rd**
Opposite Tottenham Court Rd tube station, and with a whopping selection of CDs, DVDs, videos, games and books. Occasional in-store appearances by artists plugging their latest release.

Others worth checking out

Get Stuffed
105 Essex Road, N1 (020) 7226 1364
Angel
So, it's all in very bad taste and invariably splattered in protesters red paint, but there's definitely a bizarre compulsion /revulsion type attraction to looking at stuffed, dead animals. Just you try and walk past without staring. Closed 'for a re-fit' recently amid sinister rumours.

Hamley's
188-196 Regent St, W1 (020) 7494 2000
Oxford Circus
Every child should be taken here at least once. And every adult should visit it again, alone, and without your parents telling you, you can't have everything.

Jo Malone
150 Sloane St, SW1 (020) 7730 2100
Sloane Sq
Smell the same as a super model. Jo Malone makes amazing, real, flowery scents and is the current reigning queen of gift ideas in fashion land.

The Kite Store
48 Neal St, WC2 (020) 7836 1666
Covent Garden

You never know when you might be called upon to produce an impromtu kite. Stock up while you're in the capital and never face battling with bamboo canes and old sheets again.

Lush
40 Carnaby St, W1 (020) 7287 5874
Oxford Circus
The kind of place where browsing seems more logical than buying. Natural toiletries in a lay out designed to resemble a delicatessen. Confusing.

Neal Street East
5-7 Neal St East, WC2
(020) 7240 0135
Covent Garden
A treasure trove of eastern promise. The ideal place to come for stocking fillers, comedy gifts, lampshades and kung fu shoes. And a cool place to browse if you're not actually looking for anything.

Sh!
39 Coronet St, N1 (020) 7613 5458
Old St
Northern girl done good with sex shop erotica for girls. Only accompanied males of the species will be admitted.

Soccer Scene
17 Foubert's Place, W1
(020) 7437 1966
Oxford Circus
The nation's favourite sport in shop form. Full of twelve year old boys pestering their parents for new Arsenal kits. They'll regret it when they're older. Definitely best avoided at weekends.

In a city where most bars and clubs have a door policy that reads gorgeous, it's nice to know help is at hand...

Hair

Burnette Forbes
15 Wells St, W1 (020) 7580 5006
⊖ **Oxford Circus**
Central London afro hair specialists. Also offering Aveda 'pricey but worth it' products and treatments.
Mon 10-6, Tue 10-8, Wed 10-6, Thu-Fri 10-8, Sat 9-6
Men £20/Women £45

Cuts
39 Frith St, W1 (020) 7437 4571
⊖ **Leicester Sq**
How can a barber's become the coolest place in town? When Fran Healy comes in to get a 'fin', (the style was created here) and sparks a trend across the nation. That's when.
Mon-Fri 11-7.30, Sat 10-7
Men and Women £25

Essensuals
34 Southampton St, WC2
(020) 7240 4090
⊖ **Covent Garden**
The younger, trendier version of Toni & Guy, offering modern hairstyling that looks just as good when you dry it yourself. And given the pumping bassline in the background every time we've called up, a weekend warm up into the bargain.
Mon-Fri 10-8, Sat 9-7
Men £26/Women £34

Fish
30 D'Arblay St, W1 (020) 7494 2398
⊖ **Oxford Circus**
Trendy, Soho hair salon always abreast of the latest trends in hair world. Also has a branch in Top Shop at Oxford Circus.
Mon-Wed 10-7, Thu 10-8, Fri 10-7, Sat 10-5
Men £28/Women £33

Mahogany
17 St George St, Hanover Sq W1
(020) 7629 3121
⊖ **Oxford Circus**

This award winning salon is the choice for hair in London. Mahogany produce catwalk shows and photographic shoots all over the world – and it shows. So whether you want to look like Nick Moran or Erin O'Conner (both clients themselves) this is the place to go. Cutting and colouring in a stylish salon with a head massage to die for.
Mon-Tue 10-6.30, Wed-Thu 10-8, Fri 10-6.30, Sat 10-5
Men and Women £43

Beauty

Tanning Shop
16 St Anne's Court, W1
(020) 7434 1941
⊖ **Tottenham Court Rd**
It's not big, it's not clever and if you believe what fashion magazines tell you it's desperately unstylish. Still, everyone knows that a few hours of ultra-violet radiation make anyone look better - and hell, we're all going to die eventually. Might as well make sure you look bronzed at your funeral.
Mon-Fri 10-8, Sat 11.30-6.30
1 hour worth of stand up sessions £45
(5 mins equal to 20 on a normal sunbed)

NYNC
17 South Molten St, W1
(020) 7409 3332
⊖ **Bond St**
Broken a nail? Accidentally applied a shade of fuchsia that doesn't quite match your outfit? Help is at hand. Virtually any nail related problem, disaster or requirement can be fixed here. Thank the good lord for that.
Mon-Fri 9-8, Sat 10-7, Sun 11-5
Manicure £15

The Refinery
60 Brook St, W1 (020) 7409 2001
⊖ **Bond St**
Only in London eh? Well, here you have it, a men only spa. Women are outlawed, massages, facials and hairdressing are

you've tried this one...now try them all — **17 other cities to indulge in**

order of the day and there's not even anything dodgy going on. Most of the men I know are only just coming to terms with the concept of two-in-one shampoo and conditioner, so it must be full of boy bands and rich business men.
Mon-Tue 10-7, Wed-Fri 10-9, Sat 9-6, Sun 11-4
Treatments start at £10

The Sanctuary
12 Floral St, WC1 (0870) 0630 300
⊖ Covent Garden

Women only spa featuring saunas, steam room, treatments and a baffling array of swimming pools. The ultimate in relaxation, definitely somewhere to buy your mum a voucher for next Christmas. Not ideal for girls who can't handle more than four hours without vodka.
Mon-Tue 10-6, Wed-Fri 9.30-8, Sat 10-6, Sun 10-6, Evenings Wed-Fri 5-10
Day m/ship £58 Evening m/ship £35

Health Clubs

Holmes Place
Plaza Shopping Centre
120 Oxford St, W1 (020) 7436 0500
⊖ Oxford St

Classy gym with exercise rooms, personal trainers and a beauty salon. Part of a chain – many of the other branches also offer swimming pools, steam rooms, restaurants and basically anything else you could ever want, but they must be expensive because no-one wanted to tell us the membership price.
Mon-Thu 6.30-10, Fri 6.30-9, Sat 9-8, Sun 10-6

Fitness First
59 Kingly St, W1 (020) 7734 6226
⊖ Piccadilly Circus

Good value gym with branches across the capital. This particular example is open 24hrs during the week, so if you fancy pumping iron at 4am there's nothing to get in your way. They also offer a free video rental service for chilling out afterwards.
Opens Mon 6.30am until Fri 10pm, Sat 10-8, Sun 10-6
Annual membership £390

Tattoos/Piercing

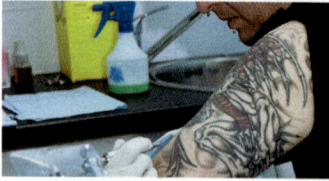

You can mutilate your body in a number of places, but be warned, there are a number of shocking operations out there run by deranged junkies with shaky hands. Camden has the most per square mile. For piercing, try **The London Piercing Studios** on Chalk Farm Road (020) 7482 4200, where all holes come with a year-long guarantee. For tattoos, **Into You** come highly recommended, at 144 St John Street (020) 7253 5085. And for absolutely the best, get to **Sacred Art** on 148 Albion Road, Stoke Newington (020) 7254 2223. Yes it's miles out, but when your Celtic band looks like a nasty case of gangrene, you'll regret not having made the effort.

accommodation

www.itchycity.co.uk

Prices are for single/double room. if you get stuck, you're best bet is to call the London Tourist Board accommodation booking service on (020) 7604 2890. £5 booking fee, Mon-Fri 9.30-6. Sleep well.

Expensive

Berners Hotel
10 Berners St, W1 (020) 7666 2000
⊖ Oxford Circus
£186/256

Covent Garden Hotel
10 Monmouth St, WC2 (020) 7806 1000
⊖ Covent Garden
£190/£220

The Metropolitan
19 Old Park Lane, W1 (020) 7447 1047
⊖ Hyde Park Corner
The best reason for staying here, unless you're already pop-star, is that you'll get admission to the Met Bar - quite simply the toughest door in London to crack.
£230/£290

One Aldwych
1 Aldwych, WC2 (020) 7300 1000
⊖ Covent Garden/Charing Cross
Unique and relaxed with a cool bar.
£275/£295

Mid-priced

Annandale House Hotel
39 Sloane Gardens, SW1 (020) 7730 5051
⊖ Sloane Sq
£60/95

Fielding Hotel
4 Broad Court, WC2 (020) 7836 8305
🚇 **Covent Garden**
£76/100

Luna Simone Hotel
47 Belgrave Rd, SW1 (020) 7834 5897
🚇 **Victoria**
£35/55

Ridgemount Hotel
65-67 Gower St, W1 (020) 7636 1141
🚇 **Goodge St**
£32/48

Royal Adelphi Hotel
21 Villiers St, WC2 (020) 7930 8764
🚇 **Charing Cross**
Bed and breakfast £50 pp

Elizabeth House Hotel
118 Warwick Way, SW1
(020) 7630 0741
🚇 **Victoria**
Bed and breakfast £30 pp

Curzon House Hotel
58 Courtfield Gardens, SW5
(020) 7581 2116
🚇 **Gloucester Rd**
Bed and breakfast £35 pp

Budget

To stay at YHA you'll need a membership card, which also doubles as handy ID for under-age drinkers.

Ashlee House
265 Gray's Inn Rd, WC1 (020) 7833 9400
🚇 **King's Cross**
From £13pp in 16 bed dorm (low season) £15pp (high season)

City of London YHA
36 Carter Lane, EC4 (020) 7236 4965
🚇 **St Paul's**
£19-£26 pp

Oxford St YHA
14 Noel St, W1 (020) 7734 1618
🚇 **Oxford Circus**
£20.55-21.80 pp

St. Pancras YHA
79-81 Euston Rd, NW1
(020) 7388 9998
🚇 **Kings Cross**
£23 pp

International Students House
229 Great Portland St, W1
(020) 7631 8300
🚇 **Great Portland St**
From £10 pp

accommodation

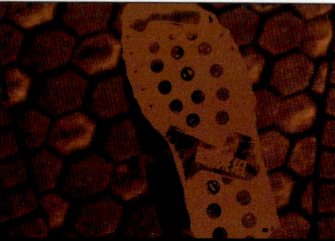

getting about

www.itchycity.co.uk

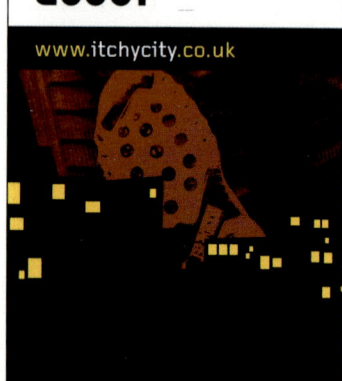

Taxi

Official London black cabs. Can also be hailed on the street, if they're in the mood and you're going in their direction.

Radio Cabs
(020) 7272 0272

Private Hire

Private hire vehicles are not officially allowed to let you hail them in the street. But thank God they do, or none of us would ever get home after midnight. Ask around the area you're in to try and identify a reputable firm. Agree and haggle the fare before-hand – usually you can knock about a third off.

Specialist Private Hire

Lady Cabs
(020) 7254 3501
For a guaranteed female driver. This service is for women travelling by themselves, not a mobile dating agency.

Freedom Cabs
(020) 7734 1313
Gay cab company.

Not minicabs

London offers an alternative take on the getting home pissed situation, namely totally random characters posing as minicabs. Usually they'll have some kind of hanging air freshener on the rear-view mirror and complain about losing their license if they take five of you, to make you feel things are a bit more authentic. This is a nice touch. Not recommended for lone females or anyone really. But they provide an essential service and novel adrenalin rush of a journey home.

London Transport

For information on buses, night buses and the tube. (020) 7222 1234

Bus

Victoria Coach Station
164 Buckingham Palace Rd, SW1
(020) 7730 3466 ⊖ Victoria

National Express
0870 580 8080

Train

Docklands Light Railway (020) 7918 4000
Eurostar 0870 518 6186
GNER 0345 225225
National Rail Enquiries 0845 748 4950
Virgin Trains 0345 222333

Planes

Heathrow Airport 0870 0000 123
Gatwick Airport (01293) 535353
Stanstead (01279) 680500

Boat

For hop-on, hop-off Thames services.

Circular Cruises (020) 7936 2033
Catamaran Cruisers (020) 7987 1185

Car Hire

Avis 0870 590 0500
Budget 0800 181181
Hertz 0845 755 5888

Tube tips

Ah, the sweet smell of sweaty armpits, jostling around in over-crowded tubes. Few newcomers to London take to the system with the blind confidence it requires, so here's a few handy tips:

- Strike up conversation with your fellow passengers. No-one else does but someone's got to buck the trend.
- When someone shouts 'Move down please!', feel free to shout back, 'Not for you, lard-arse!'. Again, most people just shuffle up without looking, but it's worth a crack.
- If a busker comes along and you don't want to give any money, try screaming 'LA LA LA' over the top of their tune.
- Taking the stairs at Covent Garden tube station may seem a good idea in the height of a stuffy underground summer, but it's not. No matter how fit you are.
- Holding up the tube doors for your mates will result in at best, a telling off from the guards, and at worst, death.
- Standing on the right on escalators isn't an optional pleasantry.
- Getting pissed and sleeping on the last tube 'til the end of the line is not recommended. At High Barnet, walk right out the station 500 yards to the cab rank on your left. Deep breath and regret.

getting about   145

index

Listings	Page No.

19:20	66
100	83
192	98
333	64
1997	121
10 Tokyo Joe's	34
25 Canonbury Lane	95
606 Club	95
93 Feet East	63
ABC Piccadilly	112
ABC Shaftesbury Ave	112
Abigail's Party	6
Accommodation	142
Admiral Duncan, The	108
Africa Bar	24
Agent Provocateur	129
AKA	29
Alba Pizzeria	85
Alfred Bar & Restaurant	38
Alphabet	7
Al's Bar Café	68
Amber	7
Ambient Soho	135
Aquarium	64
Arch 635	80
Argyll Arms	11
Arsenal FC	122
Assaggi	104
Astoria, The	110
Astral	116
Atlantic Bar & Grill	45
Atlas	135
Babushka	72
Bah Humbug	77
Bamboula	77
Bar and Dining House Islington	55
Bar Aquda	108
Bar Gansa	44
Bar Italia	121
Bar Rumba	40
Bar Solo/Under Solo	45
Bar Vinyl	45
Barbican Screen	114
Baze II Baze	73
Beach Blanket Babylon	96
Bear & Staff	37
Beauty	139
Bibo Cibo	25
Bierodrome (Islington)	51

Bierodrome (Clapham)	81
Black Market Records	135
Blue Elephant	92
Boardwalk	8
Bonafide Studios	121
Bonjour Vietnam	92
Boxfresh	132
Bradley's Spanish Bar	18
Brick Lane Beigel Bake	121
Brick Lane Market	128
Bricklayers Arms, The	61
British Museum	117
Brixton Snooker	115
Brixtonian Havana Club	73
Browns (Shop)	132
Browns (Club)	31
Browns Labels for Less	132
Buffalo	133
Bug Bar	73
Bull's Head	104
Busaba Eathai	13
Caberet of Angels	116
Café Boheme	121
Café de Paris	40
Café Delancey	47
Café Juice Bar	74
Café Naz	61
Café Pacifico	29
Café Sol	81
Camden Brewing Company, The	46
Camden Head	53
Camden Market	128
Camden Palace	49
Camden Snooker Cntr	115
Candy Bar	110
Cantaloupe	62
Capital Club	31
Cargo	64
Chariots Roman Spa	111
Charlton Athletic FC	122
Cheers	37
Chelsea FC	122
Cicada	68
Circle Bar	81
Clapham Grand	87
Clerkenwell House	115
Club 414	86
Club Gascon	69
Coach & Horses	11
Cock Tavern	20
Coins	97
Columbia Road Flower Market	128
Comedy Café	117
Comedy Store	117
Compton's of Soho	109
Constitution, The	47
Cork and Bottle	35
Covent G'den Wine Bar	25
Crazy Larry's	95

Crown and Anchor	28
Cuba Libra	55
Curzon Soho	112
Curzon Soho Bar	35
Debenhams	126
Denim	25
Design Museum	118
Detroit	26
Diesel	131
Digress	8
Dish Dash	21
Dogstar	74
Dragon	58
DTPM@Fabric	110
Duffer of St George	131
Duke of Edinburgh	75
Eagle, The	67
EasyEverything	122
Eclipse Lounge	89
Eco	85
Edinboro' Castle, The	47
El Rincon Latino	85
Elbow Room	51, 115
Elec Showrooms	60
Electric Ballroom, The	49
Embassy	51
Fabric	71
Falcon, The	84
Faun & Firkin	38
Filthy McNastys	54
Fish!	105
Fitzroy Tavern	20
Fluid (Farringdon)	67
Fluid (Fulham)	93
Food For Thought	30
Fox and Anchor	69
Foyle's	135
Freedom Brewing Co	28
Freedom Café	109
French House	12
Fridge Bar	78
Fridge Club	78
Frog and Forget-me-not	89
Front Room	89
Fuel	26
Fujiyama	92
Fulham Tup	90
Gardening Club	33
Garlic & Shots	13
Gastro	85
Gate, The	97
George & Niki's; The Golden Grill	48
George IV	75
Get Stuffed	137
Ghillies	92
Goat In Boots	90
Golborne House, The	98
Gordon Ramsay	105
Granita	56
Great Eastern Dining	

Rooms	62
Griffin	61
Grosvenor Casino	119
Gucci	132
Hairdressers	138
Hamley's	137
Hammersmith Palais	106
Harrods	127
Harvey Nichols	127
Havana	93
Health Clubs	140
Heaven	110
Helter Skelter	135
Herbal	64
Hippodrome/Equinox	41
HMV	136
Hobgoblin	76
Hogshead	38
Home (Leicester Sq.)	41
Home (Hoxton)	62
Hornimans	86
Hoxton Square Bar and Kitchen	59
HQ's	49
Ice House	52
Illicit Drinking	17
Indian Akash Restaurant	38
Intrepid Fox	12
Islington Bar	102
Itsu	13
Ivy, The	30
Jerusalem	19
Jigsaw Menswear	132
Jo Malone	137
Joe Allen	30
Joe's Basement	122
John Lewis	127
Jongleurs	117
Joseph	133
Joseph Sale Shop	133
Junction, The	79
Kabaret	15
Kensington Place	99
Kerala, The	21
King and Queen	21
Kings Head Theatre	54
Kite Store, The	137
La Perla	26
La Porchetta	56
Lab	8
Ladbroke Piccadilly	119
Langley, The	26
Legless Ladder	91
Light, The	63
Lighthouse	52
Limelight	42
Liquid Lounge	97
Livebait	31
Living Room, The	75
Loaffers	82
London Clubs Casino	119

146

London Dungeon	118
London Transport Museum	118
Long Bar	19
Long Island Iced Tea Shop	27
Loop	23
Lord Nelson, The	116
Lord's	123
Lunasa	89
Lunasa	89
Lush	137
Lux Cinema	114
Madame Jojo's	16
Madame Tussaud's	118
Mahogany	139
Mango	129
Mango Rooms	48
Manto Café	109
Manzi's	38
Martini's	45
Mash	22
Mass	79
Match	19
Medicine Bar	52
Met Bar	102
Metro Cinema	112
Midas Touch	25
Millennium Dome	118
Ministry of Sound	106
Mint	67
Miss Sixty	129
Mister CD	136
Monarch	47
Monte's	105
Moon Under Water	38
Moro	69
Mother	59
Mr Wu	39
Nag's Head, The (Covent Garden)	28
Nag's Head, The (Islington)	54
National Film Theatre	114
National Gallery	116
National Portrait Gallery	116
Natural History Museum	118
Neal Street East	137
Newman Arms	21
Nike Town	131
Nine Golden Square	39
No7 Guest House	111
Notting Hill Arts Club	101
Oblivion	82
Odeon Leicester Square	113
Odeon Mezzanine	113
Office, The	23
Offspring	133
Oh Bar	46
Old Explorer, The	21
Old Queen's Head	54
On Anon	35
Opium	9
Osteria Basilico	100
Oval	123
Oxfam Originals	132
Oxford Arms, The	47
Oxygen	8
Paradise by way of Kensall Green	98
Passione	22
Paul Smith	133
Pepper Tree, The	86
Petticoat Lane Market	128
Pharmacy	100
Phoenix Café	77
Pie2Mash	49
Piercings	140
Player, The	9
Plug, The	79
Po Na Na Fez Club	95
Poon's	39
Pop	9
Pop Boputique	132
Popstarz@the Scala	110
Portobello Market	128
Prince Albert	76
Prince Bonaparte, The	98
Prince Charles	113
Princess Louise	28
Propaganda	9
Prowler Store, The	111
Public Life	60
Punch and Judy	29
Queen Mary	104
Rainforest Café	39
Rasa	58
Raymond's Revue Bar	116
Real Greek, The	63
Reckless Records	136
Red Cube	36
Red Lion	61
Red or Dead	131
Redbacks	107
Retox Bar	27
Riley's American Pool & Snooker Club	116
Ritz, The	40
Riva	106
River Café	106
Riverside Studios Cinema	114
Rock Garden, The	33
Rock	107
Ronnie Scott's	16
Royal Mail, The	55
Ruby in the Dust	99
Ruby Lounge	103
Saatchi Gallery	117
Saffron	93
Saint	27
Sak	9
Sally Clarkes	100
Salmon & Compasses	53
Sand	82
Santa fe	53
Satay Bar, The	78
Sauce barorganicdiner	48
Scala	110
Schnecke	56
Selfridges	127
Sequel, The	83
Serpentine Gallery, The	117
Sevilla Mia	20
Sh!	137
Shakespeare's Head	12
Ship	104
Shoeless Joes	103
Shopping	124
Sister Ray	136
Six Degrees	10
Slug and Lettuce	91
Smiths of Smithfield	69
Smiths Sale Shop	133
So:uk	83
Soccer Scene	137
Social, The	20
Soho Spice	14
soletrader	133
Souk	31
Sound	42
Southern Cross	91
Spearmint Rhino's	116
Spigan	14
Spitalfields Market	129
Sports Café	36
Spot	28
Steam	103
Stepney Snooker Club	122
Strada	57
Strawberry Moons	36
Stream Bubble & Shell	71
Stringfellow's Cabaret of Angels	33
Subterania	101
Sugar Reef	14
Sun	84
Sun & Thirteen Cantons	12
Suzy Q's	116
Tate Britain	117
Tate Modern	117
Tattooists	140
Taxis	144
Telegraph, The	76
The End	31
Theatres	114
Three Kings Of Clerkenwell	68
Tiger Lil's	86
Tiger Tiger	36
Tinseltown	122
Titanic	10
Topshop/Topman	131
Tottenham Hotspur FC	122
Toucan	12
Tower Records	136
Trade @Turnmills	111
Trafalgar Tavern	104
Transport	145
Turnmills	71
Twickenham	123
Two Floors	10
UCI Empire Leicester Square	113
UGC Haymarket	113
UGC Trocadero	113
Upper St Fish Shop	57
Urban Outfitters	131
Velvet Room	107
Vibe Bar	60/114
Victoria & Albert Museum	118
Village Soho	109
Villandry	23
Vingt Quatre	90/122
Virgin Megastore	136
Voodoo Lounge	42
Wag Club	16
Wagamama	15
Walthamstow	123
Warner Village	
West End	113
Waterstone's	135
Wessex House	87
West Central	109
West Ham Utd	122
Westbourne, The	98
White Bear, The	68
White Cube	117
White Horse, The	91
Wimbledon	123
Windmill on the Common	85
WKD	46
Woody's	101
World's End, The	47
Yesterday's Bread	132
Yo! Below	11/67
Yo! Sushi	15
York, The	55
Zara	129
Zoo Bar	37

index

147

itchycities

www.itchycity.co.uk
18 delicious flavours to indulge in

for life outside london (it does exist) check out itchy's sparklingly entertaining guides for 18 uk cities on the internet, wap and in print.
to get hold of a copy, visit your local quality bookseller, or call 0113 246 0440 and we'll sort you out.